MW00638372

TWO MAYORS AND A LAWYER

THE GROSS FAMILY IN ALLENTOWN HISTORY

To John
All my best !
Mal Gross

MALCOLM J. GROSS

Dedication

This book is dedicated to my wife Janet,
and to my family,
especially our children and grandchildren from all sides,
because as Janet says,
"they are the future."

Why Study History

"There is little that is more important for an American citizen to know than the history and traditions of his country. Without such knowledge, he stands uncertain and defenseless before the world, knowing neither where he has come from nor where he is going. With such knowledge, he is no longer alone but draws a strength far greater than his own from the cumulative experience of the past and a cumulative vision of the future....

The future arises out of the past, and a country's history is a statement of the values and hopes which, having forged what has gone before, will now forecast what is to come."

—John F. Kennedy

Two Mayors and a Lawyer

TWO MAYORS AND A LAWYER

THE GROSS FAMILY
IN ALLENTOWN
HISTORY

MALCOLM J. GROSS

Published by Lehigh County Historical Society, Inc.
Lehigh Valley Heritage Museum
432 West Walnut Street, Allentown, PA 18102
http://www.lchs.museum

ISBN 978-0-942165-09-8

© 2013 Lehigh County Historical Society, Inc.
Printed in the United States of America

Introduction

I begin at the end. It's a rather odd start to an introduction. Nevertheless, it has been my experience that readers want to know where the matter ended before they really dig into the whole story.

So, first a bit about me ... For two decades, I have been happily married. My wife Janet and I have seven children between us and ten grandchildren and more on the way. I continue to practice law as I have since 1966. I also continue to represent clients, rich and poor, in courts and counties throughout Pennsylvania. I still enjoy doing it.

As for me, I was born in Allentown, PA on October 2, 1940 and grew up at 115-1/2 (yes half) Seventeenth Street across from Allentown High School. However, I attended all Catholic schools because my mother Agnes was Catholic. Until Gross family tradition claimed me for Lutheran Muhlenberg College at age 18, I was a Catholic schoolboy.

Altogether, I have been around Allentown for more than seventy years. There is a one-year interlude as a teenager when we moved to Harrisburg. I lived at Villanova while attending law school, and I spent a year in Scranton with the Pennsylvania Supreme Court. Even during those years, I returned home virtually every weekend. Allentown is where I am from and where the Gross family has been from since 1750.

I was a law clerk to Chief Justice Eagen of the Pennsylvania Supreme Court for a year. My year with the court is covered in part of this book, as is my first year of practice. It isn't as if those two short years were all there is to my life and career, but those years did more to shape me and my view of the legal world than all the others. As Justice Eagen's law clerk, I had the opportunity to work for an outstanding jurist, still the best I have ever known after many years practicing law before many men and women in black robes. Brilliant and fair, Michael J. Eagen was also kind and gentle, the perfect foil for a young blundering lawyer/clerk. The relationship I formed with him, his family, and admirers has continued to sustain me to this day. Traveling around the state with the Commonwealth's highest court and its justices, staying at fine hotels at the bargain "judicial rate," which Judge Eagen somehow got for me, as well as getting near governors and senators and the biggest names in the state bar, was exciting but also frightening.

Then, in 1966 my first real year of law practice brought me crashing down from those Elysian heights to what the late Lehigh County Judge Kenneth Koch called "the pit" of criminal practice. There, first as a voluntary public defender (read unpaid), then a county public defender (read $5,200 per year), I came to know the cops, aldermen, justices of the peace, hookers, conmen, robbers, dopers and several killers who populated the underbelly of our community. I already loved the law, but as a public defender I started a lifelong love affair with courtrooms and the action that oozes out of them into your veins. Since then I have done virtually every type of law, though today I concentrate principally on civil litigation. The excitement I feel walking into a courtroom has never left me. When it does, perhaps then, I will call it a day.

I ran for Lehigh County District Attorney in 1971 and 1975. And I lost twice. Although I got within a few hundred votes of winning, I always felt my runs for DA were an attempt to compromise my love for the law and the demand that being a Gross put on me to serve in some type of public office. Compromise doesn't work in politics or law. Campaigns were good for my career and terrible for my personal life. Political campaigning is not for me. I like people, but I don't like asking them to vote for me.

Perhaps that's why I put my efforts into the community after 1975. I have served on virtually every non-profit board and committee over the years, or so it seems. My calendar over the past four decades would reflect meeting after meeting, committee after committee, board after board. I don't know how much good I did for those organizations, but I did what I could. I am proud of some of the things I helped to get started – Wildlands Conservancy, Community Services for Children, Lehigh Valley Child Care and proud of having served as president of the Allentown Symphony and the Lehigh County Historical Society. I think and hope I did some good there.

However, all of those things were secondary to my legal career, which grew slowly but did grow. I spent sixteen years as a part-time solicitor to the Office of Children & Youth working on the side of the angels (or social workers as they are officially called) to try and save battered and neglected children for their sake and society's gain. That took me into court maybe 200 times a year. I believe during those years in the 70s and 80s Lehigh County OCYS did a great deal of good. I was proud to have been part of that good.

In 1976, Paul McGinley and I founded Gross McGinley with an office first at 137 North Sixteenth Street, and now in Crown Tower on Seventh Street as well as offices in Easton and Emmaus. Not exactly coast to coast, but today we do employ more than 60 people including 30 lawyers. The firm has an excellent reputation throughout eastern Pennsylvania. A law firm is something of an institution when it lasts as long as ours and symbolizes high quality, as I believe we do.

Three other items: First, I have represented various newspapers and occasional TV stations all around eastern Pennsylvania advocating for First Amendment rights, Right to Know laws and Sunshine Acts. I hope those efforts have done something to broaden all of our protection as citizens and open up our government. In short, I hope they have advanced democracy.

Second, I have served for 13 years as one of the five Trexler Trustees. As a lawyer, I was tremendously honored when all of the judges of Lehigh County elected me to that board which has distributed over $100 million to our city and local charities since it came into existence. As Trustee, I have tried to use the influence of the Trust to help those who couldn't help themselves and advance our county's interests.

Third, of all I have written, I have most enjoyed occasional commentaries which *The Morning Call* has published over the past 25 years. I hope they demonstrate a moderate liberal philosophy applied to the issues of the day. I have included some of them in this book because they say a lot about me and what was happening in our country and county during those years.

Finally, some observations about Allentown today. This part is perhaps the most difficult and risky because the past is fixed, the present here, but who knows the future of Allentown or anything else. It's like trying to describe the rushing waters in one of those parks my grandfather loved so much.

However, I can say Allentown is today truly a "city" and no longer a "town." Its language is as much Spanish as English. Its schools are as much a mix as a United Nations' meeting. Its politics now revolve around disconnected sometimes alien groups, not the city fathers who promoted Mal

Gross for Mayor in 1920. Even its cuisine is now on a wide spectrum from Turkish to Caribbean. How can you guess how such a stew will taste in 20 years?

Nevertheless, that's how a city works, and Allentown is looking to be a great city. Its population is over 117,000. It's growing again like it did in the 20s. It is truly the cultural center of the Lehigh Valley with its fine museums, library, and colleges, most of them forming a cluster right downtown, a stone's throw from the home of my parents when Jack was Mayor in the 60s. Now it also looks like a major sports arena will be added to go with Allentown's new baseball stadium, all drawing people here from all over the Lehigh Valley the way Hess's did fifty years ago. So there is hope, as there was when this all started when "Mal" was first elected over ninty years ago.

Huge cranes are moving gigantic slabs of wall and floor as the arena takes shape before my eyes. Perhaps more important, massive new office buildings and apartment complexes are also being built in the same area. To look down Hamilton Street from 9th or 8th and see the cityscape being transformed from a series of derelict early 20th century buildings into modern skyscrapers is really quite incredible. The visions of Malcolm W. Gross, and the tragically interrupted efforts of John T. Gross are now on the verge of being fulfilled. There is still much to be done. Allentown's poverty rates and blighted neighborhoods are shocking and discouraging, but at least something new has started here. Allentown is rising again as it did in the 1920s and 1960s.

And here I am still trying to carry on some of the traditions my family has established in Allentown. The roots of those traditions are found in what follows.

Malcolm J. Gross
Allentown, PA
December, 2013

Editor's Note

In this book, one of Pennsylvania's most distinguished attorneys reveals his deep connections to history. Malcolm Gross was born in Allentown, the third largest city in the Keystone State. His grandfather and later his father served as mayor of the city.

The first three chapters of this book take the reader back to Allentown in the 1920s, the Great Depression, and later to an era of powerful economic growth. It tells the story of political struggle, disappointment, and triumph. This is history told by a writer whose father and grandfather lived through extraordinary times. It is a story of how Allentown functioned, matured, and rose to prominence. The first chapter is completely new. The next two chapters were previously published in the *Proceedings of the Lehigh County Historical Society.* Collectively, they tell an important story of American political and social history.

Most of the other articles were authored as op-eds for *The Morning Call,* a regional newspaper with wide circulation in the Lehigh Valley. The original publication date of each article is part of its title. These essays represent an important cross-section of American culture and historical commentary. Frequently they deal with turning points in U.S. history, from Lincoln's Gettysburg Address in 1863 to Thomas Jefferson, and the "Limits on Free Speech;" every topic makes its point in a unique and relevant way.

To a current reader much in this book reveals popular discourse from the past. The op-eds reveal important topics that were subjects of debate and commentary during the years in which they were written. In that sense they tell us as much about the past as the writer who wrote them. They explore important topics that remain relevant in our day.

With the exception of minor editing and slight title changes, the op-eds appear as they did when they were previously published. We thank *The Morning Call* and *Pennsylvania Lawyer Magazine* for permission to reprint them in this book.

Joseph Garrera, Executive Director
Lehigh Valley Heritage Museum

Acknowledgements

We achieve few accomplishments in life without our friends, and this book is no exception. Foremost, I must thank my wife Janet for always being available, for listening to my stories, and for enduring never-ending history talk.

My good friend and former newspaper editor Ardith Hilliard took an early look at parts of this book and made great suggestions. My dedicated administrative assistant Elizabeth Minger worked tirelessly in what were some of the most lengthy typing assignments of her career.

Jill Youngken, Assistant Director of the Lehigh Valley Heritage Museum gave up a complete weekend to re-read the entire manuscript. Her help was appreciated and significant. Others from the Heritage Museum dotted i's and crossed many t's. Josh Fink, Carol Herrity, MaryAnn Seeko, and Sarah Thayer re-read important parts, offering helpful suggestions.

Henry F. Ballone, graphic artist extraordinaire, laid out the book and fused the chapters together. I am extremely grateful for his assistance.

Kieran McAuliffe, graphic artist and citizen of the world who created the facinating cover for this book.

Along the road of life, I am constantly inspired by my many friends and colleagues. No doubt, I have forgotten a name or two. I can only say that I am inspired by, and grateful for, your support. It goes without saying that any errors in this book are my own.

Malcolm J. Gross

Table of Contents

M. W. Gross – The Beginning, the 1920s, the Crash

This was intended to be the third and final, article on my father John T. Gross and grandfather, Malcolm W. Gross terms as Mayor of Allentown. The first two appeared in the <u>Proceedings of the Lehigh County Historical Society</u> and are republished here. The Society ceased publication of the <u>Proceedings</u> some time ago, so that I am publishing the third article in this book to complete the sequence.

My first memory was at age three or four because my grandfather Mal died in 1944. I was in a small middle room of a long house, and a tall gaunt man was sitting in a black leather wing chair. Somehow I had been told, or sensed, that this man was important, that he was almost a demigod. My second early memory is being taken to another man's garage or was it a work shed and seeing a nearly completed bust of the tall gaunt man. My third memory, in 1947, was being required to pull a string of a drop cloth so it would fall off and display that bust in the Allentown Rose Garden. A band played, and I was very frightened. In fact, I was frightened on each of those early occasions which is perhaps why I remember them so vividly.

Those memories are my only living connection to Malcolm W. Gross, my namesake, who was Allentown's mayor in the 20s and 30s. He was the dominant person on the local political scene in both of those important decades in Allentown's history.

The gaunt man, a wing chair, and the stone face projected an almost awful sense of dignity. My mother, Agnes Lieberman Gross, was herself a formidable figure, but once remarked that Malcolm W. Gross was the "most dignified man" she ever knew. In fact, she never called him anything but "mayor" throughout her whole married life.

Gravitas has always been a crucial attribute for America's public officials. George Washington was the model for it. He was once described as having, "quitted the room with a dignity so severe that every person seemed alarmed." Mal either consciously affected the appearance of dignity or it came naturally to him. For whatever reason, it was one of his critical links to Allentown during the city's golden years of the 20s and desperate decade of the 30s. Somehow Mal was the personification of a mayor. Somehow his silent stare was more powerful than many of the now forgotten voices around him.

The Lehigh County political scene had numerous aldermen, councilmen, burgesses, and even judges. That said, Allentown had only one mayor, and there was only one Allentown. Perhaps it was natural that the overwhelmingly Pennsylvania Dutch community in Allentown during those years gave automatic deference and respect to its mayor. Germans have a great reverence for authority. Perhaps it was simply his ability to survive in the difficult political climate of those twenty years. For whatever reason, Mal's "dignity" played a role in making him what he was. So did the newness of the city, its people, and its government.

It was Mal who saw and seized on that newness. The form of Allentown city government changed drastically a few years before Mal took office. He seemed to understand that change gave the opportunity to an ambitious politician to make the office of mayor something new and significant. He did that in many ways, but perhaps most important among them was the way Mal carried himself as the city's mayor. At some point as a boy, I recall being shown joke books with Pennsylvania Dutch humor which he apparently had used in his speeches. Yet, I can never recall hearing anyone say he was a humorous man or that he even liked to laugh. From early childhood there is no picture of him smiling. Instead, his image was always serious. Nor was he ever photographed with a cigarette despite the fact he was a chain smoker. Only a man sensitive to his public image realized the permanent effect a photo would have.

He was not handsome; which is not to say he was ugly. However, as a prematurely bald, very tall thin man he looked nothing like the jut-jawed, slicked-backed hair, arrow shirt man of the 20s poster. His appearance was always a careful balance. He never appeared in either the outdated winged collar or the new sportier casual outfits of his decades. Unsmiling, he always appeared in a vested suit with a tie, very much the picture of a serious 1920s banker, lawyer or public official.

Three things strike you immediately about Mal. His height (which was anywhere from 6'3" to 6'6" depending on which news account you read), his bald dome, and his penetrating black eyes exaggerated by bushy black eyebrows. Mal's baldness arrived early. Photographs of him as a young lawyer already show him with it advancing relentlessly.

Mal must have been worried about baldness. In 1897, a local newspaper reported what it regarded as a hilarious incident. Mal's thinning hair had apparently concerned him to the point that he went to a barber in Bethlehem for a "treatment" designed to restore hair loss. The treatment, most likely consisting principally of alcohol, was rubbed into his head after which he made the mistake of lighting a cigarette causing his scalp to erupt in flames. The damage was not serious enough to keep him out of action for more than a few days, but the embarrassment of the publicity must have been enormous to a young man trying to create an image of dignity. That kind of public flap never happened again.

Was he born dignified? Photos in the late 1890s don't give a viewer the picture of the subject's inner workings. They were always posed, not candid. Those of Mal show a young boy and then a college student with those same dark eyes and bushy eyebrows. With a full head of hair Mal had a more dreamy and romantic appearance. But he remained serious. Regardless, romantic or dignified, there was always something deeper and older about Mal than his fellow students at Muhlenberg College. Even his college nickname was "Old Abe."

He came from respectable, if not prosperous, local stock. His ancestors arrived in the Lehigh Valley from Germany via Philadelphia in October of 1753. From that time forward, they apparently found a home in Allentown where they worked at various trades and small businesses in the tiny borough. Henry Gross, Mal's great-great grandfather, served in the militia during the American Revolution. Another ancestor fought in the War of 1812. Then the family seemed to have fallen on hard times. They lost their goods and property on Allen Street at a sheriff's sale in 1819. Thereafter, the family history is blank until 1854, perhaps the result of the embarrassment of the 1819 failure, until 1854 when Mal's grandfather Charles, a butcher, was elected as Lehigh County Recorder of Deeds. Either then, or at some time earlier as they wandered in the wilderness of insolvency, the Gross family had found politics as a safe haven – Democratic politics.

Charles died in office in 1856, and his son George succeeded him. George Tilghman Gross, born Christmas Eve 1829, served honorably in an Allentown regiment during the Civil War. His education only consisted of having worked in a print shop as a young man. However, he held a long string of government jobs apparently due to his Democratic Party connections. He was a revenue collector, prison inspector, and court crier. He was elected twice to the Assembly, and probably his most important position was being appointed Postmaster of Allentown by Grover Cleveland in 1888. Postmaster was a powerful position, controlling a significant number of patronage jobs for letter carriers. He was also Democratic chairman in various local and state election campaigns. George was renowned for his knowledge of election statistics and ended his work life operating a tobacco shop at a local hotel. He may also have had a problem with "the bottle" according to a family story.

Malcolm Weickel Gross, George's and wife Elizabeth's only child, was born October 14, 1872 and grew up in Allentown. George's salary as Postmaster probably provided enough funds to send Mal to Muhlenberg, the first member of his family to attend college. Mal graduated in 1894, and moved away from Allentown for the only time in his life to take a position as a railroad clerk in Perth Amboy, New Jersey. After a time in that job, Mal returned to Allentown, and probably through George's influence, was placed in the office of Judge Edward Harvey where he read law and was admitted to the Lehigh County Bar in 1899. Thus, Mal was not only the family's first college man, but he was its first professional.

Mal quickly followed George into local Democratic politics. He was elected and served a three-year term as Register of Wills. Trusts and estates seemed to have been his principle interest as a lawyer outside of municipal work. In 1908, he was chosen as a delegate to the Democratic State Convention, and in 1912 he attended and was one of the "sponsors" of a large local rally for the Democratic presidential candidate Woodrow Wilson at the Lyric Theater in Allentown.

Lehigh County politics in the decades before Mal became mayor in 1920 were very much in a state of flux. The county's Pennsylvania Dutch had voted Democratic since Andrew Jackson in the 1830s. After the Civil War, there was a gradual movement by the middle class to the business oriented Republican Party, especially in Allentown. Samuel McHose, a relative of the Gross family and Allentown's first mayor in 1867, was a Republican who changed parties after being horrified by a slave auction he witnessed. General Harry C. Trexler, the city's most prominent citizen, was a Democrat until 1896 when he left the party over the free silver issue in the McKinley – Bryan election.

Mal's interest in national or even state politics was minimal throughout his career. His support of Wilson in 1912 may have played a part in his appointment to the city draft board during World War I, but that was hardly a significant position. He did show enthusiasm for Al Smith, the Democratic candidate for president in 1928, and seemed to begin taking more of an interest in national politics after that time. However, with Republicanism on the rise in Allentown, overly enthusiastic support of the Democratic Party would have been politically dangerous.

In 1910 Mal's legal and political career reached an important milestone. He was elected city solicitor by the old ward-based city council after several ballots in a hotly contested election. When Mal became solicitor the city had a population of fifty-one thousand. Only ten years later the population increased to seventy-three thousand. By the time he left office in 1932, the population leaped to ninety-six thousand. Allentown had two blocks of paved streets in 1900 and ninety-one miles of paved streets in 1931. From 1920 to 1932, the city's size had expanded from twenty-one hundred to forty-three hundred acres. The change in Allentown was a great deal more dramatic than its population numbers and acres. In the years after 1920 when Mal was first elected mayor, Allentown became a true city - a more diverse and complex community.

Almost all of this change occurred in the fabulous decade of America's Roaring 20s. The Roaring 20s was actually a "short decade" in Allentown. In the first five years of Mal's terms as mayor, the city was still struggling from the effects of the aftermath of World War I on the American economy. The city, attempting to deal with its rapid growth, put in place a form of government which could make the new city work. At the same time, the gasoline-powered autos, trolley cars, electrified houses, and businesses, telephones, radios, and daily newspapers almost suddenly became embedded in every Allentonian's daily life. With these inventions came an economy built on consumerism, salaries, and hourly wages, rather than agriculture.

None of these social trends and inventions was new in the 1920s. All had been around for decades. The first gas-powered auto was built in Allentown as early as 1889. However, autos and other wonders of the new consumer economy had not been part of the common man's everyday life until the 1920s. Their impact was felt only when they worked together. They had to complement each other to create the effect they did on Allentown. That effect was possible only if people were crunched together in a city. The compactness of a regional city of twenty- five thousand to one-hundred thousand people, like Allentown, was critical to their powerful but short range.

No highways existed on which the new Model T Ford could be driven, but Allentown's miles of new paved city streets made its daily use possible in-town. The countryside lacked electricity, but wiring a small compact town like Allentown was relatively easy. Powered by electricity and gasoline, inventions like the auto, radio, telephone and home appliances became useable.

A city required a full time responsible city government. Allentown had no such thing in 1910 when Mal became solicitor. The cumbersome bicameral, part-time council based on election by each city ward was dysfunctional and parochial. Although the title of mayor existed, the office lacked any real power to govern or administer the city. Except for the city engineer and solicitor, there was no professional city staff to direct the bureaucracy.

That changed when state law permitted a new city charter. As city solicitor, Mal literally wrote that charter at the last minute in 1915 when the council was unable to get its act together to do so itself. The result was a new form of government with the mayor and four councilmen acting together as a real "city council." Each member of the council had a vote and sole responsibility for a particular part of city government. The idea was that an elected official would then also have specific accountability for the performance of his department. However, the new mayor-council form of government had an unintended consequence. The council, chaired by the mayor, was more like a board of directors needing a majority to take any action for a budget or legislation. On the other hand, the day-to-day operation of the city's streets, police and fire departments, etc., was run by individual councilmen. Yet, each needed funding from an overall city budget and city ordinances to permit them to administer their departments. That meant that the council had to govern by consensus and arrive at a commonality of goals to permit each department head to function daily. Al Reichenbach, the city's first new mayor under the new charter, was elected in a non-partisan election. With his health already failing Reichenbach seems to have looked back to the old days of a mayor being only a title rather than a platform for action. Thus, things were much the same as in the old days until the election of 1919. By 1919, state law also began requiring partisan party elections. With Reichenbach ailing and unable to stand for another term, Mal became the Democratic candidate. Mal would have preferred non-partisan elections to continue and appears to have seen himself initially as a bridge between the city's old-line Democratic voters and the surging tide of new local Republicans.

As a result, Mal played down his Democratic credentials in the campaign and kept quiet about national politics. There was nothing to be gained by a local Democratic politician attaching himself to the then unpopular national party of Democratic Woodrow Wilson, especially in heavily Republican Pennsylvania.

It worked! On November 5, 1919 *The Morning Call* reported that Mal had defeated Dr. R. D. Peters, the Republican candidate, by at least fifteen hundred votes. Mal was Allentown's new mayor.

Mal's successful campaign had stressed three points. First, he repeatedly called attention to his degree from Muhlenberg. Few Allentonians bothered about a college degree. Success in business was based on access to capital, shrewdness, and connections. A degree was useful only as an entry into law, teaching, or the Protestant clergy. The practical Pennsylvania Dutch saw no need for a "higher education" for success or recognition in their businesses, clubs, or farms. Nevertheless, seven previous mayors had degrees from Muhlenberg, and most others had degrees from other colleges. Apparently, the voters looked on their mayor as a professional. Muhlenberg was also very much of a commuter school in those days, so that the local alumni must have been useful as "one of their own."

Second, Mal touted his experience as city solicitor, particularly his important role in writing the new charter. As the author of the city's constitution, Mal could claim that he knew how to make the new city government run.

Third, Mal referred to a trip he had taken to the western states with former Mayor Iobst. A western journey would hardly be seen as something of note in a political campaign today. But in the early twentieth century, the West was a place of glory and mystique. A man

7

who had been there was somebody. Mal's trip made him someone different, and he turned that point to his advantage by emphasizing that he had used his time while traveling to study the "progressive" forms of western city government. "Progressive" rather than liberal or Democrat seems to have been a deliberate way Mal had of stressing his commitment to "new" ideas in Allentown while his link to the past through Muhlenberg permitted him to make that point as well.

Meanwhile, under the surface, there was also a movement by the city's power structure to put Mal in the mayor's office. There were at least two favorable newspaper articles about him in the critical month before the November election. One said, "Mal Gross has mastered the art of citizenship through practice. He has proved his worth." Another said that, "although [his] work has not been attended by any brass band tactics...he has sense enough to know and he credits voters with knowledge that taxes must be paid to provide for municipal affairs." The same paper credited him with not "boasting" during his campaign. Both news accounts had picked up on the dignified, competent, non-partisan image that Mal was already projecting in politics.

The men behind Mal's election surfaced on November 8th only days after his victory. The annual writers' club dinner featured all five of the city's living former mayors in a tribute to Mal. Former Mayor Fred Lewis was among the five. He would shadow Mal's career, losing to him in a bitterly contested 1927 election, replace him when Mal retired for the first time in 1932, swear Mal in again as mayor in 1936, and then attend his funeral in 1944. Lewis quipped, "Allentown has elected you Mal don't let it go to your head," at the dinner. The group; Schaat, Schaeffer, Hemsicker, Rim, and Lewis appeared together again at Mal's swearing in on January 5, 1920. There they presented a framed tribute to Mal wishing a "progressive administration and good health." Diplomatically recognizing the new power of city council as well, a similar tribute was presented to its members. As he was becoming the sixth of the former mayors, outgoing Mayor Reichenbach commented it, "gave him great pleasure to wind up thirty years public service swearing in M.W. Gross." All of this was hardly coincidence. The new city still had a power structure from its past.

Mal, who had linked his campaign to his deep local roots, now had a firm footing in the city's past. However, he also had a bridge to the future. Both newspapers' pre-election endorsements and the former mayors' tributes called for a "progressive" administration. Progressivism was popular with both parties. Progressive Woodrow Wilson had won the Democratic nomination with key support from Pennsylvania and had kicked off his campaign here in 1912. Teddy Roosevelt headed the Progressive ticket the same year and carried Pennsylvania. Progressivism was a powerful word. In Allentown, it was to come to mean a consensus for growth in the new decade when Progressive was very much of a spent national movement. Whatever else could be said on the issue, calling for progressive action was always a safe position in Allentown even after the Depression hit in the 30s.

Mal began to keep a scrapbook. Scrapbooks were a popular entertainment in America going back at least into the 1880s. Mal's scrapbooks were full of clippings and some official correspondence both of which reflected his ego and a remembrance of what he thought was important in his city each day. Scrapbooks lack the introspection of a diary, but they are nevertheless revealing of how he saw things going for him as well as the city. Each year of his administrations saw more large accounting ledgers pasted full of newspaper clippings and other items recording successes and failures. Many those items were about the miles of streets, sewers, water lines, and sidewalks being built by Allentown's new city government. These unsexy, but vital improvements made the new community, its autos, telephones, and electrified buildings possible. Progressivism meant that Allentown had formed a consensus necessary to raise the capital by public borrowing to finance those improvements. The label progressivism was now stretched to something positive for everyone. On March 25, 1920, the strongly business-oriented Chamber of Commerce even called for "conservative progressivism" in government.

Mal's scrapbooks also told a story of the personalities involved in developing that "progressive" consensus. But from the beginning there was opposition to the new direction he was steering Allentown to. First disputes surfaced between the new mayor and city engineer, Harry Bascom, an irascible city servant not cowed by Mal's public outbursts. Bascom gave as good as he got, mostly complaining about shortages of money in his department, weather, and other problems beyond his control. Soon rival personalities on council arose as well and so did citizen and political opposition. But in the long haul of his 16 total years in office, Mal dominated the political scene.

Mal's fame as mayor of what was rapidly being called the "Queen City" of the Lehigh Valley, was aided tremendously by the growth of the new phenomenon of the daily home delivered newspaper. Soon that newspaper also contained photographs of local officials. Photographs probably did more than anything else to spread and cement Mal's fame. Local news completely dominated the newspaper in the 20s, and the new communities were starved for that local news. The city's new residents craved connections to the strangers around them. The daily newspaper supplied that and photographs, much like today's television made people believe they were directly connected with the city's officials as well. Of course Mal also knew that he needed personal contact with the voters. He did that by simple gestures such as walking to work daily and having an open door policy at his office. But the daily newspaper, with its photos, made Mal relevant to all Allentonians each morning and evening, and he faithfully clipped every story about him good or bad.

Mal's long, sad face was somehow perfect for the photographic image. His height also fascinated Allentonians at a time when most men were a foot shorter. The newspapers favored photos of groups of prominent men that inevitably emphasized Mal's height as the tallest of the group. Even earlier in 1909, local cartoonists, who satisfied the public's urge for pictures before newspaper photography was perfected, showed Mal sledding with his new son, Jack, with an extra pair of wheels behind the sled to accommodate his long legs. A cartoon a year later showed Mal at an Elks' picnic with an elongated body, again with his son Jack. Even with the poor quality of newspaper photographs, the daily readers must have seen their new mayor as a dramatic figure dominating the news by wedding his dignified expression and great height to the new important mayor's office.

There was a good deal more to Mal than his height. He was an ambitious young man. He had made a mark at Muhlenberg where he was class president. At his confirmation at St. Paul's Evangelical Lutheran Church in 1899 Mal chose the Gospel of Matthew 7:7, "seek and ye shall find" as his biblical inspiration. Later, as mayor, he saved an exchange of letters from a local minister who asked his idea of a successful life. Mal replied, "Success and happiness are synonymous," and cited the Greek Croesus who died nobly and was "honored greatly" as an example of Mal's idea that, "great wealth, honor, or glory" were essential to success. He never came close to attaining the first, but the second and third were his, at least within the confines of his native city.

Mal made himself the quintessential public man. For his library he favored the impressive leather bound sets popular at the end of the nineteenth century such as Alexander Dumas' historical romances, *Messages and Papers of the Presidents, The Wit and Humor of America* and *Modern Eloquence.* There is no evidence that he read any of his books, and he never mentioned anything from them in his public utterances from the records I have. But, they were exactly what the coming young man should have on his shelves.

Mal's home life is something of a mystery. In addition to his son Jack, he had a daughter Elizabeth by his wife Mable Yost whom he had married May 14, 1908. Mable and Mal met in California during his trip there. Mable's family was originally from Allentown. She was the daughter of Nevilla and John Yost, an Allentown roofing contractor, who was forced to move west because of his health. Mable apparently broke off an engagement with a doctor to marry Mal, and her parents were not happy about her doing so. There are few pictures of her. One in the early 1940s shows her drawn and sad. Although fourteen years younger than Mal, she survived him by only a short time. In fact, her poor health seemed to be the recurring theme in their marriage. In January 1930, for instance, Mal reported to the press that she was so ill he needed to carry her from place to place in their home. She appears only once in Mal's scrapbooks when she gave a lecture to a Women's Democratic group on "city government." The only other thing we know about her is that she was a teetotaler who would not allow alcohol in the home. As a result, Mal stopped daily at his beloved Elks Club to have his evening cocktail before heading home.

On January 20, 1920, shortly after Mal's swearing in, the *Evening Chronicle* reported that he had met with the entire police force and told them to look for "big things" in the city in the next five years. The first "big thing" was announced the next day. Rittersville Borough, consisting of seventeen hundred twenty-six acres, which today forms a major part of Allentown's east side, had petitioned to be annexed to the city. The physical expansion of the city's boundaries in all directions that was to supply the land for

Allentown's spectacular growth in the 20s had begun. Only a week later, South Allentown Borough with four hundred sixty-two acres followed suit bringing in a major piece of the south side.

Meanwhile, Mal began setting a tone for his new office. First he gave up power to improve the mayor's image. For years as "chief magistrate," the mayor presided as judge over police court. Mal found this role demeaning for high office. Police court was filled with loud drunks and low women swept up nightly by the city's police force. Newspapers loved to report on the court's tumult. Mal believed that the news stories about the raucous scene were degrading to the office of mayor. As a result, the same day as the addition of Rittersville was announced, he put forward a plan to have city aldermen, rather than the mayor, handle the police court. The *Lehigh Valley Review* quickly praised him, predicting he would emerge as the most powerful mayor in eastern Pennsylvania as a result of his "progressivism which would not favor any class."

March 10, 1920, Mal moved again to define his new office. Allentown silk workers had shut down one of its major industries in a strike for higher wages. Mal boldly announced he would act as a mediator in the strike. His mediation ultimately failed, and the workers stayed on strike with their demand for a thirty percent pay increase and forty-eight hour workweek. However, he had demonstrated that Allentown's mayor had the authority to act beyond city hall on major community issues. Only a week later when he and council passed an ordinance extending the city's main street all the way to its eastern boundary with Bethlehem, Mal gave a hint of where he hoped the psychological lift given by the new thoroughfare would take the city. Mal proposed the new street be known as "East Hamilton". Thus, he signaled a link to Bethlehem for Allentown's downtown.

The idea of Allentown and Bethlehem becoming one city was soon touted more overtly. At the November 29, 1922 meeting of the Four Square Club, Mayor Yeakel of Bethlehem boldly proposed a merger of the two cities and a compromise whereby the new metropolis would be named Bethlehem, and Mal would be its mayor. Cryptically, Mal responded with a biblical reference that, "a new Moses will arrive in ten years to lead the people," and asked, "Why pull away from each other?" The concept of a merger continued to be discussed throughout the 1920s. However, as Bethlehem became more and more a city dominated by "the Steel" and Allentown pointed west, not east, for its future growth, the idea of one city finally died.

Despite the upbeat attitude of its mayor, Allentown struggled with growing pains in the aftermath of World War I. As soon as the war ended the national government quickly, and not always carefully, withdrew from the local and state scene. Federal regulation of prices, wages and local affairs ended abruptly. The effects on Allentown, not yet fully sure of itself, were jarring. The silk workers' strike was one of those effects as wage controls ended with the war. Another was soaring prices. At a council meeting on January 11, 1922, Mal denounced local bakeries that were charging eight to ten cents for a loaf of bread. He claimed that bread in Philadelphia and New York was selling for as little as five cents a loaf. He proposed that the council pass a resolution referring the matter to the new Chamber of Commerce. His publicity campaign worked. Although the council had no authority to regulate prices, the council debate embarrassed local markets. Mohican Market, one of Allentown's largest, announced it would lower its price to five cents. Others followed suit.

High coal prices were also an issue. Thousands of people living in a compact city had easy access to electricity and telephone services. However, those same people were utterly dependent on Carbon County coal pits for heat. High coal prices meant serious problems for residents with no other source of fuel. Prices continued to rise into 1922, and on October 16, 1922, Mal was quoted in the *Chronicle* as having discovered that Allentown residents were being discriminated against at the pits by being charged a dollar per ton more for coal than those from nearby cities. An appeal to the Pennsylvania Coal Commission by the city, at Mal's instance, produced no results. Frustrated, he appealed directly to the governor, but also apparently to no avail. Finally, Mal set up a program to have the city police at least provide coal to the poor that was partially successful. However, because of theft and the small quantity the city could afford, it did not provide all the relief he had hoped.

Unemployment also surged in the aftermath of the war. Mal addressed the Chamber of Commerce on October 5, 1921, expressing concerns about high unemployment as well as the problem of coal for the poor. He proposed an "employment bureau" which was promptly created the next day operating at the YMCA. Within less than a week the bureau had found places to work for fifty out of the three hundred twenty-one men who registered as unemployed.

Trolley fares increased, as well, to seven cents shortly after Mal took office. He attempted to refer the matter to the public utility commission. However, the city solicitor advised that a legal fight with the commission was beyond the city's means.

With success or without success, Mal had established himself as the spokesman for the public on economic injustice in Allentown. Mal grasped that one of the intangible powers of his office was its public voice. Speeches by the mayor got instant press coverage, and press coverage could move and influence the tightly knit local community. But Mal did more than get publicity. He offered solutions. He named names. He demanded government action on problems. He quickly learned that there were limits to what a mayor could do. His mediation failed, state boards failed to act, and state law prevented him from achieving much of what he hoped to do locally. But he came to see that appearance of action even without measurable result was important to his prestige. The public came to hear his voice as their voice.

On a personal level, the mayor's three thousand five-hundred dollar per year salary gave his family a steady income, and Mal virtually abandoned his private law practice. He still attempted a few cases in the estates law area, but otherwise he was a full-time mayor. Ultimately, he became so dependent on his salary that one of the themes in his 1927 campaign was that he had sacrificed his law practice for the city and needed a job as a result. However, in 1920, his new income made him confident enough to buy a farm in Weisenberg Township for fourteen thousand dollars as a summer home. He raised sweet corn and entertained the city's police at summer picnics there and at another farm he rented in future years. Since he never learned to drive a car, the city sedan and driver, which came with the mayor's office, were yet another advantage of his new job. Howard Nonnemacker, his cousin, was the faithful chauffer with a nominal position in the police department.

Within a few days of acquiring his new farm, Mal's son Jack was in Allentown Hospital with one of his many life threatening childhood illnesses. Jack's health was so bad that he became disabled, and ultimately he, his mother and sister temporarily moved to

California in the hope that a warm climate would benefit the boy's weak lungs. Mal lived alone for that time, and the combination of loneliness and the pressures of tumultuous events of the early 20s may have led to a depression. In June of 1920, praising the new truck industry at Mack, he predicted that Allentown would be the third city in Pennsylvania in "a few years," but also said, "I may not live to see the day." Immediately after, he sold the farm at a substantial loss and then on August 9, 1922, at the opening of the Central Park swimming pool, after predicting that Allentown and Bethlehem would come together under one "management," he said again that, "we may not live to see it." Finally, only three weeks later, *The Morning Call* quoted him as saying, "if I didn't hate like Sam Hill to desert a sinking ship, I'd resign my job."

Mal's constant sniping battle with the city's engineer Harry Bascom also continued. Bascom became the symbol of all Mal's frustrations. As early as April 1920, Bascom had leaked a story to the *Leader* newspaper about the necessity of "economy" in the street building program because prices had doubled after the war. Mal struck back with an attack on the "feed" to newspapers from public officials. On April 19, 1920, he followed up with a vote by council to "censure" Bascom for allowing a fence on Center Square during construction. In May, Bascom was almost not reappointed until Mal, following what was to become one of his most fixed principles, deferred to councilmen Ruch, Bascom's supervisor as head of the streets department, and voted for his retention. Disputes with Bascom continued as Mal often lost patience with what he saw as the slow progress in street construction particularly East Hamilton Street which Mal called "a death trap."

By the summer of 1922, the argument between the two men again flared into the open when *The Morning Call* reported Mal demanded, "this job should be rushed" and Bascom exploded, "it is not my fault." Finally, in late August, Mal again saying he was on the verge of resigning, summoned Bascom before city council, and sent what must have been a pointed message to Councilman Ruch when he made clear that the flip side of his support for each councilman's control over his own department was that Ruch was responsible if the department failed. That outburst was the high tide of the dispute. On September 7th, Mal announced he was determined to have

Seventeenth Street finished for the Allentown Fair. Then Mal rallied. Paved streets apparently did it. There is something about street construction that is tangible when it comes to measuring progress. You can see it happen block by block. By September 11th, the *Chronicle* reported the city set a record for paving in one day. Even the use of concrete was sacrificed to asphalt to get the city streets paved, but not without a near breach of Mal's budding alliance with General Trexler. Harry Trexler's principal company was Lehigh Portland Cement, and Allentown was known as the "cement city." However, asphalt was favored for city street construction by most experts because it was cheaper and easier to apply. Nevertheless, Councilman Kohler fought a final battle for local cement. Mal countered that the "experts" favored asphalt. Kohler hit back with "don't dare holler at me." Regardless, Mal's view prevailed, and construction went forward with asphalt. Somehow, Mal still managed to preserve his relationship with the General.

With the concrete controversy over, assistant city solicitor Harold Helfrich reported that in 1922 Allentown now had 45 miles of paved streets. Mal told *The Morning Call* that no previous year in the city's history had seen so many improvements launched.

Then on October 21st, Mal, now triumphant, spoke to the Loyal Order of Moose saying, "I feel that the only way you can accomplish anything is to thoroughly saturate yourself with the thing in mind – dream it, think it, and talk it…it takes leadership." Only five days after his speech to the Moose, the newspapers reported that he spent Saturday at his desk. It was his birthday, and he seems to have given up all thought of resigning.

1923 was a bridge year for Mal and Allentown. First, it was election year for mayor. Great successes in 1922 had set the stage for the coming campaign. Ed Lumly, a local businessman, emerged as Mal's Republican opponent. Apparently referring to Mal's growing connection with General Trexler, Allentown's most prominent Republican, Lumly claimed that Republicans had difficulty finding a candidate because of the high cost of campaigning. This was an apparent reference to the General's financial support of Mal. Lumly campaigned on the slogan of "he wears no man's collar," and that he was opposed "to invisible government". Lumly's campaign made public the ongoing quiet relationships that had been developed between Mal and powerful Republican business interests like the General. But Mal not only had the General's silent backing, but the public endorsement of the Labor Trades Council as well. As a result, he won a crushing victory with a majority of almost 7,000 votes, carrying the entire city and sweeping two Democrats, Bartholomew and Guth, onto city council with him. Lumly had apparently been ill during part of the campaign, but he himself recognized that his health made little difference. In a concession letter to Mal he noted the mayor's "popularity" and joked about his own "remarkable unpopularity."

Apparently emboldened by his win, Mal, speaking to a Democratic women's group, was quoted in the *Record* newspaper as predicting nothing but Democratic victories in the future. 1923 was the first time Mal had faced women voters, and he obviously had done as well with them as with Allentown's men. He had cultivated their votes a year before the election when he spoke to the Women's Club asking for their support for home rule in Allentown government.

Mal's confidence in future Democratic successes was misplaced. He spoke at the high-water mark for Democrats in Allentown in the 20s. As the city developed and the roaring 20s legend arrived in 1925, Mal and the Democrats struggled against a growing Republican tide. In 1920 Democratic presidential candidate James Cox had managed to stay within seven thousand votes of Republican Warren Harding in Lehigh County. In 1924 Coolidge's margin over John Davis was more than ten thousand, and by 1928 Herbert Hoover obliterated Mal's candidate Al Smith by twenty-seven thousand votes.

In the face of Republican dominance, Mal managed to win a close reelection victory in 1927 over Fred Lewis. But either he was determined to stand by his now strengthened Democratic beliefs or he simply wasn't getting it right politically. His first misstep had been an attempt to have himself elected delegate, one of the two, to the 1924 Democratic convention from Berks/Lehigh. Mal genuinely wanted to go to the convention in New York City. In a statement he said he would support a "progressive" presidential candidate, not making a commitment to any particular one. However, he also hoped to launch himself as a candidate for Congress from the congressional district in 1928 by winning in 1924 as a delegate. The Berks County

Democrats who controlled the congressional seat had other ideas. They sent a message to Mal by electing two Berks residents as delegates. Mal lost by fifty-seven votes. It was Mal's first and only election defeat. Today, it seems minor in an extremely successful political career. However, it must have been a bitter lesson about the limits of Mal's political reach because my father still talked about it thirty-five years later. Mal was trapped in the mayor's office. His legal practice was gone, and after the 1924 loss there was nowhere else to go in public office.

Although there are fleeting references through the years in Mal's scrapbook of efforts by unnamed "friends" to run him for congress or even governor, he never seems to have seriously considered leaving Allentown politics again. He would give his all out support to Al Smith in 1928, even writing to the national committee with suggestions about the "farm problem," but he was now mayor and nothing more or less than mayor for life.

Meanwhile in 1927, Mal survived a razor-thin election win for his third term as mayor. Trexler's financial support and the hardcore Democratic organization in the first and sixth wards carried him through. But it was a victory with a price. Mal and the Democrats were branded by the Republicans as having stolen the election. Consensus government on council was replaced by political factionalism and a surging Republican strength.

A central issue in the 1927 election had been the dramatic increase in the city's tax assessment, which had been blamed on a Democratic controlled city council. The Democrats, on the other hand, blamed the increase on "errors" in the assessor's office. Retaliating, John Yingling, the chief assessor, had been "titular campaign manager" for Fred Lewis against Mal according to the press.

Immediately after the election, Yingling needed reappointment by the council. Mal was put in a box. For his first two terms he had faithfully followed his rule of allowing each member of council to appoint his own department heads. Yingling's office was under the control of Republican George Cavanaugh. Yet Yingling had led the election campaign against him. The situation was further complicated when new Republican Councilman Hohman wanted to replace two men in his department. The press quoted unnamed Democrats as threatening, "if Hohman desires to start something there are others who can finish it but not to his taste." The consensus that had been nurtured by Mal over the years was in real danger of being torn apart.

Worse, Mal's close call in the recent election had weakened his hold on the remaining Democrats on council. By January, Mal's position was clearly crumbling. A "rumor" had it that the police department would be transferred by council from Mal's jurisdiction. That may have been a result of a 1927 scandal in the department that had been another issue in the 1927 campaign. Control of the police was one of Mal's sources of power and dignity. His response indicated both the seriousness of the threat and his isolation. Instead of relying on the nominal Democratic majority on council, he pointed to state law that required the police department to remain under the mayor's control. He and Democrat Roth then failed in an effort to have former Councilman Bartholomew appointed to a vacancy on council and saw Republican Weiller named instead. Mal did, however, salvage one thing. Yingling withdrew as a candidate for assessor, but Republican John Rhin was named to his job by council. Mal swore Rhin in with Councilman Cavanaugh looking on.

A new pattern had been established in Allentown government. Republicans were, in effect, in control of the city for the next forty years until the mayor-council form of government ended. Despite winning the mayor's office seven more times, and occasional control of city council as well, Democratic Party discipline was so weak that success came only through individual accomplishments by Democratic mayors. City hall was never to be a power base for the Democrats as it was for the more disciplined Republicans.

Party politics aside, three seemingly insignificant issues were to continue to appear and reappear throughout the balance of Mal's terms in the 20s. In an odd sense, they defined Allentown in those years. Daylight saving time, prohibition, and baseball, each, in their own way, exposed real fissures in the growing and changing community. Old and new values were in plain view, and city government was the focus for the battles.

Daylight saving time demonstrated the clash of national American ideals with the reality that America was essentially a country of local communities. Once World War I ended, people looked again to their local governments for solutions to their problems. However, some issues left over from the war stubbornly stayed there. Of all things, the seemingly innocuous concept of daylight saving time caused a bitter split in Allentown. Instituted during the war to save electricity, it gave city dwellers an extra hour of daylight in the summer. However, the farmer hated it because it disrupted his morning work schedule. The issue surfaced April 8, 1920; the council passed a resolution to "voluntarily continue" the wartime measure in Allentown. Apparently aware of the political dangers the measure posed, Mal opposed it on the ground that it would "confuse the issue." In February of 1922, the council again voted in favor of the daylight saving time in the city. Again Mal opposed the resolution unless it was "universal," meaning adopted for the whole country. Mal had found a political strategy to avoid a fight. As with a number of issues in his career, he was able to take the position that right or wrong, the thing was beyond the control of the city government. Time and again, in what would become an annual debate, Mal noted that Allentown was really at the mercy of the state and national government on daylight saving time. It could not set up its own time zone and continue to be part of the nation's expanding commerce.

Yet the issue remained throughout the 20s. Nine years later, Councilman Roth forced a resolution through the council banning daylight saving time in the city. By then, daylight saving time, thanks mainly to the railroads, was virtually a national norm. Again Mal tried to avoid the issue claiming that the state already had taken the power from the council to put it into effect. Roth answered that he was "bitterly opposed to daylight saving time," and the resolution passed. Problems immediately arose when police shifts ignored the resolution and other city employees protested because it would interfere with their "social lives." By April, Roth noted the whole city government was working on daylight saving time, except his own department. *The Morning Call* described him and his protest as being met by "grim silence" by his colleagues. Ready or not, daylight saving time had come to Allentown by default.

Baseball, and particularly Sunday baseball, presented an even more graphic example of conflicts between the old and new. Mal had played baseball at Muhlenberg and continued his interest after college. He even kept a clipping about him playing first base at a Bar

Association picnic in 1920 while he was mayor. Connie Mack, legendary owner of the Philadelphia Athletics, was a good friend. Yet baseball, particularly professional baseball, had a dark side. As America's first great professional spectator sport, it had become a lucrative business in the early decades of the twentieth century. But in 1919, it was rocked by the Black Sox scandal in which a World Series was fixed by gamblers. Professional baseball was seen as corrupt and corrupting to its fans. On the other hand, amateur sports were seen as good and wholesome. On November 10, 1922 trying to make a case for the amateur, Mal spoke to a city athletic banquet. He praised Hugo Bezdek, the Penn State football coach who was paid ten thousand dollars a year, but had recently turned down a much higher offer from the Philadelphia Nationals Football team. Mal told the young audience they should have the same ambition, by which he seems to have meant, to rise to the top of amateur sports, but disdain making more money from the professionals. When the city first leased the Fairgrounds for summer activities, a project Mal had heavily promoted working for the first time with Trexler, the Fair Association demanded provisions in the lease banning Sunday baseball. Professional Sunday baseball was a particularly sore point with some because it involved money and the Sabbath.

Meanwhile, baseball continued to grow in popularity, and when Yankee superstar Babe Ruth cancelled a trip to Allentown in May 1922, Mal went to New York personally to try and change the Babe's mind. He failed, but was praised by the local press for his efforts.

By the start of the 1924 season, professional baseball was a fact of life in Allentown. However, mainline Protestant churches still didn't want it played on Sunday. On May 9th, at one of the largest meetings of its kind in the history of the city, ministers passed a resolution demanding a ban on Sunday professional baseball. The Protestant Women's Federation followed with a similar resolution the same day.

On May 17th, Mal announced that, "there shall be no commercialization of the Sabbath in our city." The arrest of "Duke" Langraf, the Allentown Dukes manager, followed that Sunday's game, for violating the Blue Laws that banned commerce on Sunday. The complexity of what seemed a straightforward issue quickly became apparent. The Blue Law Act of 1794 was not clear as to which court has jurisdiction over the arrest. Police Magistrate John H. Berneche dismissed the case as being brought in the wrong court. Worse, Berneche announced that, "if the law was enforced at all, gas stations and stores needed to be closed as well as some churches who have paid organists." The decision and comment were greeted with loud applause by the audience. The chief of police was required to quiet the crowd.

Embarrassed, Mal met with the Federation of Church leaders three days later to find a way to stop what he continued to call the "commercialized Sabbath." He ordered new arrest warrants for each Sunday the law was violated with the case directed to the correct court.

Meanwhile, opposition to Sunday enforcement continued to mount. The Seventh Day Adventists passed a resolution against the Blue Law. A public opinion piece in *The Morning Call* pointed out that a garage directly across from City Hall was open Sunday, and that *The Morning Call* itself was violating the law with its Sunday newspapers. There was a deeper level to the issue as well. Allentonians worked a five and a half day week. That essentially left only Sunday for fun and spectator sports. The working man wanted Sunday baseball and professionals provided the best quality game.

Regardless, the limits of law as a remedy to enforce moral codes on the modern world soon became clear. The fine for violation of the Blue Laws was four dollars. Baseball managers promptly announced that there was no need for a hearing. They would voluntarily pay the fines every week. The Federation talked of an injunction, but took no further action beyond a more generalized resolution against "commercialization" the following year.

The Dukes were soon established as an Allentown institution when they toured Puerto Rico the next winter spreading the city's fame. Mal accepted an autographed baseball from the entire team and preserved it next to one with Connie Mack's signature. Once the Dukes became part of the campaign to boost Allentown, the charge of "commercialization of the Sabbath" vanished. The Federation of Churches retreated to ask only that there be no paid concessions in public parks on Sunday. On February 5, 1925, Mal put a new twist on the issue. He challenged local baseball clubs to join in building a large stadium. Mal hoped to turn the divisive issue into a way to give the city a new venue. No stadium was built then, but the seed was planted for the School District's construction of a massive J. Birney Crum Stadium two decades later.

Finally there was Prohibition. It came to symbolize the roaring 20s in America. Essentially, Prohibition was an attempt to impose a morality judgment of progressivism on the country by a constitutional amendment. As with the ban on Sunday baseball, it had the wholehearted support of the Protestant church, but not all other Americans.

Prohibition became the law of the land January 16, 1920, only a few days after Mal took office. The full extent of the problem of enforcing this sweeping new moral code was not fully appreciated. It was assumed that, as they had with so many wartime regulations, the public would simply comply with a good thing. It took a year, until early 1922, for Mal's clippings to even reference the issue. The federal government had only 1,520 men to enforce the law in the whole country. As enforcement became a problem, it was assumed that community cooperation and local police would make the law effective. Neither of these assumptions was likely to work in heavily German beer drinking Allentown.

Trying to avoid the problem, the city's police department that Mal headed soon adopted a policy of enforcing the law only against public drunkenness by rationalizing that the sellers to those drunks were out of town "foreigners." That myth ignored the fact that the drunk was buying liquor sold in Allentown. Still, even when the police did make an arrest of the seller, the press used it as an opportunity to blame the stranger. On February 2, 1922 local newspapers reported that a still run by Thomas Beiss "claiming to be a Russian" was raided as the source of "hooch." A month later Lehigh County district attorney Richard Iobst announced that drunks would be questioned as to the source of their liquor and sellers prosecuted. However, after a raid on one or two speakeasies, efforts quickly were transferred back to arresting the drunks. In 1923, Allentown police arrested 319 persons for public drunkenness, compared to 196 in 1914. Another 153 people were arrested for disorderly conduct as opposed to 73 in 1914.

Chief Bernhard acknowledged that the problem was the unenforceable law, but continued to blame the crime it spawned on immigrants. In an interview with the *Record* on June 4, 1922, the Chief acknowledged that the city's crime problem was worse:

> I attribute it directly to Prohibition. I would rather handle ten of the old drunks then one today. When a man gets drunk on the rot gut stuff pedaled by our foreign bootlegger he is a crazy drunk. My experience shows that ninety percent of the bootleggers are foreign unnaturalized immigrants. The fruits of our having prohibition are being gathered by our foreign element.

Except for reporting that the city's arrests for public drunkenness had risen to over 300 per year, Mal's scrapbook says little about Prohibition for several more years. Then on January 16, 1924, Chief Bernhard suddenly surfaced and issued an order to his department to clean up the city. Charging that liquor was being sold at fifty cents per glass at "the biggest clubs in town," and that crime was festering in city speakeasies, bawdy houses, and gambling dens, the chief demanded action from his police. Only days later, however, the *Lehigh Valley Register* asked whether the police will also, "clean up - themselves?" It quoted people familiar with Allentown affairs as charging that the police were in on the illegal activity.

As with District Attorney Iobst's efforts against the speakeasies, nothing more was heard of the chief's campaign against illegal liquor. The problem, however, continued. On May 18, 1927, it reached highest levels of city officialdom when Fire Chief William Kranzly was suspended and asked to resign on the charge of intoxication.

By 1928, Mal had come to accept the failure of Prohibition as a fact of life, but claimed it was having little effect on his city. He admitted to a Philadelphia newspaper, which called him "Milton W. Gross," that:

> I think things are in pretty fair shape here....It has been a long, long time since I saw a drunken man on a street in Allentown. I venture to say we are no better or worse than any city our size. Seventy percent of our population is of Pennsylvania German descent.

They were always drinking beer and saw nothing wrong with doing so.

Despite Mal's claims that he saw that no drunks, Allentown police had arrested 919 of them in 1929. And a local newspaper reported in a non-scientific poll taken about the same time that 4,920 voters considered themselves, "wet" and only 1,405 "dry," When federal revenue agents tried to shut down Hauk's Bar on Linden Street near City Hall for selling illegal booze, a mob surrounded the bar. The trapped federal agents called City Hall and asked the mayor for assistance. Mal was alleged to have answered, "the federal government made this law let them enforce it." Mal and Allentown had come to a bargain (perhaps a corrupt one) to live with Prohibition as long as its worst effects were not publicly displayed. Whether that arrangement would have worked indefinitely will never be known. In 1932, the Democrats and Franklin Roosevelt finally swept into office, and Prohibition was gone shortly thereafter.

If prohibition, baseball, and daylight saving time demonstrated the clash of old and new values in Allentown in the 20s, home ownership and the automobile symbolized the new world of that decade. The car's vital role in Allentown's life was demonstrated on January 1, 1924. As part of its New Year's edition, the *Chronicle* reported home building, like never before, with 59 new homes under construction and 500 completed by the end of the past year. Mal promised the building boom would be helped by the city's employees, "We will work with both hands. Less than 100% percent staff work will be taboo at city hall." All of those new homes, and many more, were apparently inhabited by citizens with cars. In 1923, 493 new homes were built, and 551 garages went up as well. In 1926, 758 new homes were built supported by 785 private garages, and, as a gesture to the past, one stable. The pattern of a house on the street and a garage in the alley was established in Allentown.

The advantage of auto travel on the city's new streets had one major negative effect - cars killed. In 1926, twenty people died in car accidents and two more from auto and trolley crashes. Three more were killed by gunshots and ten by bad hooch. Deaths from auto accidents declined to 15 in 1929, but 532 people were injured. Worse, four children were killed in those accidents and another 198 injured.

The city's response to the rash of car accidents was to add more police. In 1924, the police department added 20 new men and put 10 new motorcycles on the streets. Jaywalking was prosecuted, and safety campaigns started in the schools. Mal ordered no parking on Hamilton Street. Eventually, however, regulations and technology solved some of the problems. In April 1925, the traffic light arrived and was tried on Hamilton Street and soon appeared elsewhere in the city. Technology replaced more manpower as a solution, as it has done so often in our day as well.

The additional police budget, however, could not accommodate women officers despite the Women's Club's lobbying for a female cop. Mal assured the Club that the request would be "considered," but apparently did nothing more. A newspaper cartoon showed a woman officer locked out of the department.

Radio had also become a major part of daily life. On October 5, 1927, the *Chronicle* reported that three thousand people packed the Manhattan auditorium to see a display of new radio receivers. Mal was the principle speaker. He noted radio's power and unifying effect on the county. "Radio is one of the greatest forces of our generation. It performs an invaluable service in saving human life, crops, and property." It "unites the people of a country in a common interest," he said.

Allentown saw still more major events and successes before the 20s ended. In 1927, College Heights became part of the growing West End. Mal noted, "Strangers enter Allentown through beautiful environs and that will mean Allentown's reputation as the city of charm and cleanliness will be greatly enhanced."

On September 19, 1927, Mal got an ovation from the crowd as he dedicated the new Americus Hotel saying, "I have never had any doubts about our ability to maintain such an institution." The massive construction site, before the new hotel, had furnished a background for the famous photo of Mal and Harry Trexler several years earlier. The Mayor and the General in straw bowlers, an incongruous Mutt and Jeff dignity and panache, somehow symbolized the 20s in Allentown.

On January 9, 1930, Hamilton Park added yet another 310 acres to the city. Mountainville, with South Fourth Street, joined the city as well. However, the devastating effect of the stock market crash three months earlier was already hitting Allentown. Eight days before the Hamilton Park annexation, the city laid off thirty-one employees despite Mal's brave statement that, "no other city in the state will do as much progressive work in 1930 as Allentown." Mal still clung to the magic word, "progressive" to inspire his city. But, the Great Depression that was rapidly gripping the city and country was beyond words.

By September, the Family Welfare Association announced it was no longer able to provide charity and food to the city's poor and that 200 families were dependent on that charity. At the same time, a "large industry" was about to close according to Mal. He said, almost in despair, "We have tried to keep it…out of the circle of publicity. What will happen in the fall?"

In March of the following year, 50 men gathered to demand relief from the city and action from their mayor. Police refused to "get excited" according to the local press. But police bravado was not enough to silence fear and anger.

By fall of 1931, a socialist party rally at Center Square drew 500 angry men. The police had broken up an earlier attempt. Apparently sensing the need for an outlet for anger, Mal personally told the crowd he was "entirely willing" to have the men use the square. Then 200 unemployed men marched directly to City Hall. Police were needed to guard the doors. Finally, a committee of three that was led by Frank Fisher, a paperhanger and communist, (who the press labeled) met with Mal and demanded the city give a $1 million dollar guarantee for the unemployed, as well as free gas to the public, and lunches for children. Mal responded that the city's operations were controlled by state law. Fisher accused him of "passing the buck." The situation in America, now near revolutionary chaos, was no longer amenable to Mal's tactic of shifting responsibility to the state or federal government. Action locally, with whatever means were available, was all he could do.

In the desperate situation now confronting him, Mal first fell back on his ideas for solving the slump of the early 20s. He called for setting up a central committee on employment. The poor had always been one of his major concerns. Mal saw their situation as desperate. He set up "clothing days" in which bundles of clothes would be gathered at city hall for the poor. He cited an "urgent need" when asking for help. He told the Civic Club that there were, "approximately 2,500 family heads affected by the present depression. This is not the time to consider who should get the credit for doing relief work. Allentown has always taken care of its needy in the past and certainly will do so now." "Depression" was now more than a word, and the city and its residents as a community had to do what they could for those in need.

Mal used WSAN radio to broadcast a call for pledges of money for the poor. Radio was no longer a novelty to send out weather reports. It was another tool to get out the mayor's message of the help needed to save the situation. He again mobilized the police department for poor relief as he had during the coal shortages in earlier years.

Working with the council, Mal also began a whole series of public improvement projects to create jobs and build the city infrastructure at the same time. The centerpiece was the Kline's Island incinerator plant using only local labor at a minimum wage of thirty cents per hour. Mal remarked, "Charity begins at home."

As his term ended, Mal pushed through completion of his last pet project. The Rose Garden capped the massive park system that he and Trexler, as head of the Planning Commission, had created in the 20s. The cost of the new garden was $29,000 and became an issue in the 1931 Mayor's campaign. Even though Mal was not a candidate, he pointed out that the completion of the project had employed forty people and that the city had grown culturally by having its own rose garden.

As always, Mal preached the practical value of improvements in the city and saw their long-range cultural merit as well. His bust still presides over his vision.

Mal's Last Term (1936-1940)

The story of Malcolm W. ("Mal") Gross's fourth and last term (1936-1940) as mayor of Allentown begins in November 1927 when Mal won a third term in a bitter, close, and questionable vote count against Republican Fred Lewis. Problems in the police department during Mal's second term (1924-1928) had put the 1927 election in doubt. One newspaper described the campaign as follows:

> Many Democrats are dissatisfied with Gross and not a few Republicans will not vote for Lewis. These nominees will have to dig in and spend some money, or get others to do it for them. The odds at this moment are for Lewis. But sentiment is not over-whelmingly for Lewis. Gross may win if his backers scatter enough money around to ward heelers and political workers. It is said that Gross is desperately in need of the job, as he has no other visible means of support. If this is true, many may vote for him out of sympathy.

On election night, Lewis, who had led all night in the vote, was declared the winner by radio station WSAN which then aired his victory speech. Meanwhile, at Mal's home on Walnut Street, he was dissuaded from conceding by his relative, Malcolm McHose, who had reportedly bet $1,000 on Mal and clung to the hope of a victory because the Democratic stronghold of the Sixth Ward had not yet announced the tally of its paper ballots. Based on McHose's encouragement that "the Sixth Ward isn't in yet," Mal withheld a concession.

At the Sixth Ward's first voting precinct, the Republican minority inspector left before the vote count was complete, and the ward's Democratic boss, Packie Cummings, could be heard in telephone conversation asking McHose, "How many more does Mal need?" after which he instructed the Sixth Ward election officials to "Count 'em again." Finally, late into the night, the district returns were reported at 420 to 71, for Mal. The Sixth Ward count had seemingly brought Mal back from defeat.

A drum and bugle corps and Democratic torchlight parade pounded down Walnut Street and filled the mayor's house to celebrate his comeback. The Republicans naturally complained of a stolen election. Yet, when the Sixth Ward Election Board was summoned into Court, it was determined that there was "no accusation of cheating." As a result, the case was discharged, and the count stood. Ironically, the whole Sixth Ward controversy was unnecessary because an error was discovered in the Ninth Ward vote, which gave Mal a majority in the city regardless of the Sixth Ward. Nevertheless, the 1927 victory was hardly something on which to build a successful third term.

Fred Lewis issued a sour concession statement:

The will of the people was thwarted by party treachery and the circulation of falsehoods. I, however, have the satisfaction of knowing that the best element in this community accorded me its support.

A newspaper offered these further comments:

The close election for Mayor is significant for one thing - the people are very much opposed and dissatisfied with the present conduct of the city government. The police force is the particular target for criticism. Things are badly managed in that department and the Mayor is held responsible. No fine city like Allentown can go forward with so many objectionable men on its police force. The vote for Mayor does not put the stamp of approval upon the present conduct of that office; rather it is a warning to the Mayor to make a strong effort to reform his police department.

The general bad feelings coming out of the 1927 election must have been particularly painful to a man of Mal's pride. His whole life had been intimately linked to his performances as mayor, and the idea that he wasn't doing his job or had not been honestly elected must have cut deeply. Mal had held public office almost from the beginning of his parallel career as a lawyer. First, he had been register of wills for the county, and then, beginning in 1912, city solicitor, followed by mayor from 1920 forward. He was a proud man and proud of his record for integrity.

By any standard, Mal's tenure as mayor in the decade of the 20s was a great success. Allentown grew and prospered. Large areas surrounding the city were annexed. Paved streets, grand parks, and public utilities went hand in hand with a real estate boom in the West End. Construction of the Pennsylvania Power and Light skyscraper made Hamilton Street the commercial center of Lehigh County, and a new industrial base emerged on the city's south side with the opening of the Eighth Street Bridge. Yet, the police problems, followed by the tainted election victory of 1927 worried Mal. Then, in 1928 he spent his remaining political capital by publicly supporting his fellow Democrat, Al Smith, in his hopeless campaign for the presidency. Although a Protestant himself, Mal resigned from local Masonic organizations because he considered them responsible for much of the anti-Catholic ugliness which tore through the county and the country in 1928.

Mal's support of Smith, especially in the form of resignations from organizations which wielded great political power, made any chance he had for a fourth term in 1932 remote. And when Mal and District Attorney Ethan Allen Gearhart appeared before the final meeting of the Democrats in Lynn Township to plead with the crowd to stand by the party and Smith, he courted political disaster. Lynn stayed Democratic, but Lehigh County went for Republican Herbert Hoover by a huge margin, and Mal's Allentown base gave Hoover a 13,128 vote majority. The latter was particularly ominous for the 1931 mayoral election.

These portents of defeat were soon joined by others. The Great Depression, which started in 1929, left the city's economy in ruins. Difficulties with the firemen made matters worse. Not surprisingly, therefore, despite support from his Democratic supporters for another run in the 1931 election, Mal announced his retirement for "health reasons." His Republican rival, Fred Lewis, then won a stunning victory on both tickets in the primary. For a Republican to win the Democratic primary, especially by defeating incumbent Democratic Councilman Brown, was a sure sign that Mal's sense of defeat, if he had run again, was correct. His public career appeared over.

Mal's leaving office in January of 1932 was hardly the end which might have been expected after twelve years of successes for the city. Little praise for his efforts appeared in the newspapers, and few congratulations came to his office. Nevertheless, Mal swore in his successor and moved into a private law practice with Robert Haas and Morris Efron. His silence in the face of adversity was consistent with the dignity which he valued so highly. No character trait stood higher for him. Of the hundreds of photos of him, virtually none show him either smiling or frowning. Instead, in each, he has almost always positioned his immense height in the center of the photo group and stared with coal black eyes and an upturned but closed mouth directly at the camera. This serious, dignified look was central to Mal's appearance at all times.

How difficult it must have been for such an awkward looking man to maintain that degree of control both on and off camera. Newspaper stories describe Mal's height as 6'3," but his gaunt face and terribly thin body made him look even taller, almost like a stick man. His total baldness, contrasted with huge eyebrows, only emphasized his great height. Mal made his looks his trademark, and so made it easy for local cartoonists to caricature him.

Matched with Mal's height and dignified look was a brevity of words which was quite different from the verbose style of politicians and particularly fellow lawyers of his day. Mal's public statements were nearly always limited to a few paragraphs or even sentences. His entry in *Men of Allentown* in 1922 is the shortest and least informative about any man in the entire book. Unlike his fellow *Men,* we learn nothing about his lodges, awards, legal career, or religious affiliation, and little about his personal life. Either he wished to create a mystery about himself or, as seems more probable, he thought it undignified for a man in high office to say much about his personal life or achievements. A few short paragraphs emphasizing his position as mayor and former solicitor are the only description of Mal.

A quiet and prosperous retirement as a senior lawyer was, however, not in the cards. No clients came to him in his new law practice in the Commonwealth building. Instead, with the Great Depression gripping the city, and before the age of pensions and social security, Mal found himself in nearly desperate financial straits.

Whether he directly approached his old friend, now Judge Gearhart, or whether friends did so for him, it must have been deeply humiliating to ask for help. Gearhart responded by convincing the Lehigh County Bar Association to create a new paid position of secretary for Mal. As a result, Mal earned $1,200 per year for keeping the Association records. He had never succeeded in law and few of his close friends seem to have been lawyers, yet the position apparently permitted him to make ends meet for the early years of his retirement.

Times continued to worsen, however, and far more successful local lawyers ended up as bankrupts or even suicides. Children's educations were abruptly interrupted in Mal's own family for lack of funds. Those same hard times did not spare Mayor Lewis. When the Dime Saving Bank, of which he was president, failed during his term of office, his popularity collapsed, making it likely that a Democrat could regain City Hall in the 1935 election.

Mal was the obvious choice to be that Democrat, vindicating his reputation and giving him the much-needed income. The mayor's office carried a salary of $5,200 per year. He apparently won the nomination without serious opposition. Few records exist of his final campaign which, not surprisingly, does not appear to have been well financed. General Trexler, the city's most powerful Republican, who had secretly supplied the money for Mal's 1927 campaign and its heavy newspaper advertising, was dead, and Mal had no money of his own.

Instead, Mal substituted personal contact for money. The Sixth Ward's Irish families were lobbied. The *Little Stick* newspaper, belonging to his friend Charlie Ettinger, pushed his candidacy. Other long-time friends aided him in other ways. Even Allentown's tiny black population was visited personally by Mal and his son, Jack Gross, asking for support.

Ettinger's paper was rewarded with one of the campaign's only advertisements. It stressed that Mal was a "Democrat." In contrast, his entry in *Men of Allentown* had notably failed to mention his party affiliation. Despite Mal's earlier avoidance of party politics, his 1928 efforts for Al Smith, and the general pro-Democratic mood of the country as Roosevelt's 1936 landslide approached, apparently made him a more committed party man as he fought in his last campaign.

A 1935 card, which was one of the campaign's other expenses, carried the usual unsmiling picture of Mal and stressed that voters should read the "facts" which are that "Mal" is a native Allentonian who has the experience to run the city. His opponent, Harry Dubbs, was not mentioned, but Mal was apparently attempting to play on Dubbs's relative youth and inexperience in not having held city office.

The election was close, and Mal trailed in the early count. Later a wag joked that Dubbs had been "mayor for thirty minutes." Mal was finally declared the winner. Despite losing, Dubbs was satisfied with the campaign, which he described as "clean" in contrast to other local elections in recent years, and congratulated Mal on his victory.

Mal's reaction to his last win was brief but emphatic and unusually personal. He described himself as "extremely happy" after noting that four years before the city had "desired a change," but that now times had again called for his return to office. Even this brief show of pleasure was quickly limited, however, and he refused to make any commitments as to policy in his upcoming administration.

In his mid-sixties, apparently in continuing poor health, and out of politics for four years, Mal might have been expected to coast through his last term. Either because he felt a need to vindicate his earlier service to the city, or because he still had the drive and vision to try to push Allentown ahead, Mal moved with dispatch and direction once he again became mayor.

Mal's fourth and last term was to be difficult because of a terrible economy, provincialism on the City Council, and the absence of some of his old allies. But he quickly demonstrated that he was determined to make his final term a statement of his principles of city government and a vindication of his previous efforts as mayor.

As the outgoing mayor, Mal had sworn in Fred Lewis four years before; now the roles were reversed and Lewis swore in Mal on January 6, 1936. This ceremony, which was invariably photographed and featured in the newspapers every four years, was obviously considered a significant statement of continuity and good sportsmanship by the press. It must have been painful for the participants. Despite public appearances, evidence of hard feelings still remained. At the first meeting of the new City Council, Mal quickly cast the only negative vote against appointing Lewis's former secretary, Alan Weinsheimer, as clerk of the Department of Public Safety. He gave no explanation for his rejection of what appeared a minor appointment. His negative vote probably amounted to a personal statement on past political disputes with Lewis and Weinsheimer. Since Mal preferred to build consensus behind the scenes rather than publicly differ with the City Council, a "no" vote on Weinsheimer's appointment reflected lingering bitterness from Mal's past contests with Lewis.

If this vote was personal, his vote at the same meeting to combine the Bureau of Parks and Bureau of Trexler Park into the Parks Department was either for reasons of economy and efficiency, or a power play to move thirty patronage jobs from Republican to Democratic control. These bureaus and their jobs shifted from one councilman to another in 1927 and must have been a political plum. Mal now proposed to move them again.

Mal had championed economy in government as one of his first principles. Gradually, however, he had to reconcile his frugality with the problem of how local government could meet the costs for new streets, parks, and utilities - needs which he also recognized. Mal solved this dilemma by gradually substituting efficiency for economy as one of his primary objectives in city government. As a result, he justified his plan for a major shift in control of the Park Bureau as being more efficient and, therefore, less expensive.

Mal's plan, perhaps not coincidentally, took jobs from Councilman Herbert Weiler in Public Safety and gave them to Mal's longtime ally, Councilman Ed German, who headed the Water and Parks Department. As a result, Weiler accused Mal of trying to "build a political machine in City Hall." German simply remarked that, "it would be a pleasure working with Mayor Gross." Immediately thereafter, Mal formally introduced his plan which won the Council's approval over Weiler's bitter objections and despite petitions which Weiler presented from his supporters. Mal then attempted to win Weiler's future goodwill by assuring him that "the transfer was no reflection on him." Weiler's response, however, made clear that in the future he would be counting votes. "It's four to one - there's nothing I can do," he said.

Mal quickly followed up to take advantage of the newly merged Parks Department. On January 21, 1936, he announced the appointment of Ernest Ashley as superintendent of Parks. Under the previous administration, the position had been vacant for two years. Significantly, Mal himself made the announcement, rather than Councilman German who was to be the new superintendent's superior. It was clear in the first month of his new term that Mal took a major personal interest in the city's park system. As always, Mal coupled his plan with the rationale that economy and efficiency made the new idea possible. Mal claimed that the savings from the recent creation of one department under German made Ashley's appointment possible because the savings of the merger covered his salary.

Coupled with Ashley's appointment came an announcement, this time by German, that the city would seek $225,000 from the federal Work Projects Administration (WPA) for improvements to Jordan Park. Mal was described as "falling into the enthusiasm of the WPA officials" for the project. Efficiency could not supply the capital necessary for continued growth of the park system. Without large city funds available, Mal was prepared to turn to other sources for the parks. As usual, however, Mal stressed that putting men to work, not improving the park system, was the chief advantage of the project. Mal's political sense was already telling him that in Depression-racked Allentown, jobs were critical.

The controversy over the Parks Department had exposed a fatal flaw in the "weak mayor" form of government exemplified by Allentown's Mayor-City Council system. Mal was proud of his role in creating this form of government for Allentown when he formulated the new City Charter in 1914. It seemed to work well during Allentown's period of prosperity with the annexation of surrounding territory contributing to the doubling of the city's population by 1936.

The 1914 Charter gave the mayor jurisdiction over the police department, but permitted the mayor and four council members to vie for control of the other city departments through ordinances passed by majority vote. Thus, since the mayor had only one vote, council members could control the other city departments, leaving the mayor with only the police under his jurisdiction.

In 1914, the ability of a majority on the Council to seize most of city government functions must have been of little importance. The city had only one small park, no sanitary sewers, and only twenty-three miles of streets. At that time, the only significant department was the police, with its ninety employees (including telephone operators and clerks), and the mayor controlled it.

Paradoxically, therefore, Mal's leadership in expanding the city's size and services in the 20s led to significant growth in such other departments as Streets and Parks. The budgets of those departments were under the control of councilmen, not the mayor. As Councilman Weiler so candidly pointed out, this growth meant patronage, and by

1936, with private sector jobs virtually gone because of the Depression, patronage meant power. Under the Charter, Mal had only the power of one vote, and departments such as Parks, Water, and Streets (where the patronage jobs were), were divided among councilmen, excluding the mayor. It was for this reason that Mal stressed "conflicts of interest" between councilmen when he proposed merging the Bureau of Parks into the Public Parks Department. He apparently hoped to free himself from Weiler's control over anything having to do with the park system by putting everything under German's department. Weiler's bitterness over Mal's action made clear that the parks would suffer in the future if Weiler had the votes.

On the other hand, the police department offered little opportunity for any creative action and was something of a political albatross. By 1936, state civil service laws prevented a mayor from firing policemen for political reasons. Yet, the power to grant rank was still the mayor's. The result was blatant police politicking in every city election, with dramatic promotions as soon as a mayor took office. Although Mal had attempted to give the impression, immediately after his election, that he had not yet considered his options on police promotions, his announcement of sweeping changes in rank as soon as he took office meant that, as was their custom, the men in blue had been active in the campaign.

Mal announced that Clarence Mensinger would become the new chief of police and named a new captain of detectives and other new captains and sergeants. Men holding those positions under now former Mayor Lewis were demoted to the rank of patrolmen and assigned a beat. A completely new police hierarchy was in place by mid-January 1936. As a small perk of his office, Mal even named Howard Nonnemacher, a family relative, as the mayor's chauffeur.

The difficulty with this use of the spoils system in the police department, however, was that the demoted officers remained on the force and could hardly have been expected to appreciate their sudden loss of position. Each newly-elected mayor, therefore, was likely to plant the seeds of his own defeat when he, as did Mal, jumped men up and down ranks on his first day in office.

Mal justified his sweeping promotions in the department by falling back on the need for economy in government. Presumably, by this he meant that because he also abolished the positions of police commissioner and superintendent of public affairs, and saved those salaries for the police department, his plan saved money. Mal's rationalization conveniently overlooked the fact that this particular economy eliminated the job of a Mayor Lewis ally, General Frank D. Beaty, the commissioner under the former mayor. Further, the wholesale changes in the department below the top two ranks were hardly necessary if Mal's objective was to save money by eliminating two positions.

Once Mal had put his changes in place, he apparently recognized the political wisdom of leaving the police department ranks alone. Nevertheless, he made no move to change the patronage system which gave the mayor power over ranking and to set standards for promotion. Apparently those subjects were too dangerous to touch. Instead, Mal began to make the police department more professional. In this regard, he returned to an idea he had promoted in his earlier administrations, the need for each officer to be professionally trained at a police academy. To accomplish this goal, Mal announced that he was considering an Allentown Police School when he made his changes in the department. As a first step, Mal proposed that the police force be trained at the State Police Academy. Mal spoke at police conventions and meetings, pushing his idea of a more professional department through better training. He also began sending selected officers to the State Police School.

Mal's approach to the police department was typical of his view of how a mayor should function. First, he recognized political realities in the election system and rewarded his supporters in the department. Along the same line, he was willing to demote, punish, and vote against those who had opposed him in the past. He shielded himself from political criticism by carefully pointing out the economy of his actions.

On the other hand, Mal had ideals concerning city government. He reduced those ideals to simple, workable, and politically attractive principles like efficiency and professionalism. He then implemented his principles where he could by concrete steps, such as instituting police training to build a professional force and pragmatically taking advantage of what might be available to further his goals, like making use of the existing State Police Academy. For the longer term he had the vision to see that the city needed its own police school, and he proceeded to use his position as mayor to promote this more complete solution to the need for professionalism. In that way, he built pressure on the Council to move toward his ideas.

Professionalism in government, generally, became a major theme of Mal's last term. His thoughts had now moved from economy, to efficiency and professionalism as the critical elements in local government. He came to realize that city government in the late 1930s had become far too complex for the version of the nineteenth-century Jacksonian spoils system that had prevailed in Allentown. Mal saw that the idea that any American could do any job was unworkable by then in a large city government. His fellow council members evidently did not agree.

Mal's public appearances were not limited to police events. The mayor was expected to be present and make an appropriate speech at the numerous conventions, dinners, and store openings which were occurring in the city and to issue appropriate statements on major events. These speeches and proclamations were serious affairs. The participants at civic events expected their mayor to play his part well and to properly honor national holidays. Mal did so. His numerous talks and statements, which he wrote himself, were thoughtful, literate, and always succinct. Some were quite eloquent. That said, Mal used these occasions for something more. He saw the mayor's office and the accompanying demands for public utterances as opportunities to educate people and to promote important city needs and projects.

As a result, in addition to police professionalism, Mal's parks now became a main theme of his speeches and interviews. He even listed "nature study" as his favorite hobby in a 1937 interview. Mal was determined to continue park growth despite what he called the "nightmare" of the Depression and lack of interest on the Council.

General Harry Clay Trexler, so often Mal's close ally in civic projects, died in 1933. Mal revived the Planning Commission, which the General had so successfully headed during Mal's earlier terms, with the idea of using it as a stimulus for park improvement. On March 5, 1936, Mal appointed an almost entirely new commission to replace the appointees of Mayor Lewis. At the commission's first meeting on March 18th, he challenged its members with the General's legacy and made numerous suggestions for new projects, keeping to his general theme of the need for planning and professionalism as the proper method of city government. With the reactivated Planning Commission, Mal identified a source of power (i.e., appointments to boards and commissions) still vested in the mayor. Once appointed, with the mayor's prodding, citizens pushed ahead on the respective boards to promote city advancement, regardless of Council's attitude. It was one way to avoid the gridlock of Mayor-Council government.

Yet, little could happen without outside help. The Depression ground on, deeply cutting city tax and other revenues. Economy, efficiency, and professionalism could not make up for a lack of money. In frustration, Mal spoke out against the State Legislature's constantly passing tax amnesty bills which enormously increased the difficulties of tax collection. He complained when the legislature made the 40-hour work week apply to city employees, because it would cost Allentown up to $90,000 and drive up taxes. Yet there was little he could do beyond complaining because the legislature was only reacting to the current hard times. With the State Legislature as a hindrance and the City Council divided, Mal turned to Washington. Mal hoped that the WPA could assist the city with needs beyond those of the park system.

Privately, he noted the results of successful WPA projects in controlling floods like the one that hit Allentown in March of 1936. Sensing that jobs were the most obvious need of the community, he constantly emphasized the number of men employed in WPA projects and the amount of money spent locally by the federal government.

Mal's emphasis on jobs rather than city improvements must have come from his good political instincts. An average of twenty-five people per day was calling on the new mayor. Mal must have quickly realized that people wanted work. As a result, he began stressing that the WPA was the answer to both this need for jobs and the city's need for public improvements.

Mal's pragmatism in regard to the WPA quickly ran into opposition when he attempted to persuade Councilman Henry K. Bauman to use the WPA to fix potholes in the city streets. Reacting with hostility, Bauman, who headed the Streets Department, retorted that what he needed was money to hire more of his own men. "I don't want them (the WPA)," Bauman made clear. Patronage and control were more important to local politicians than getting the streets repaired. Mal retreated, quickly pointing out that his idea was only a "suggestion." Such was his style, and he certainly knew that he had only one vote out of five to accomplish his many plans. He had already lost Weiler's support by taking away his patronage in the Parks Bureau, so he could ill afford to offend Bauman. The flaws in the Mayor-Council form of government made the city's effective use of the WPA difficult, and there was enough national opposition to the WPA to make it possible for councilmen like Bauman, who were nominal Democrats, to openly oppose federal programs when patronage was at stake.

Deaths and retirements among Mal's governmental allies made matters even more difficult. Ernest Ashley, the man Mal had chosen to restart the Park program, died unexpectedly on December 15, 1937. Ed German, Mal's closest ally on the Council and the councilman who headed the Parks Department, retired at the end of the 1937 session.

Nevertheless, Mal continued to stand up for his beloved parks. He cast only the second "no" vote of his last term at the last session of the 1937 Council when he voted against the city budget for 1938. He did so because $19,000 was moved from the Parks Department and split between Weiler's Fire Department and Bauman's Street Department. Clearly the Council was making a statement that parks were to be downgraded in favor of other councilmen's departments.

Without his old allies and with an additional Republican, Fred Fegley, on the Council beginning in 1938, Mal's power was clearly slipping, and his influence was on the wane. Another blow came shortly after when the new city solicitor ruled that Allentown could no longer support the WPA sewing project which had supplied some desperately needed industrial employment for the city. The WPA, regardless of the jobs it might bring, was no longer a viable legal option to drive many of the city projects which Mal supported.

Sensing that his ability to dominate events on the Council was nearing an end, Mal began to take an interest in community affairs. He accepted the position of head of the National Firms Division of the Community Chest, stressing that it was without compensation; he attended ceremonies in New York for the World's Fair, joined the Liberty Trust Bank Board, and attended the Navy Club and Muhlenberg events.

In short, he tried to enjoy his office. Yet, his inability to move city government began to frustrate him to the point of threatening his normally dignified public image. In a September 10, 1938, newspaper interview, Mal "painted a discouraging scene." He blamed partisanship and "elected officials giving jobs to friends" for government's problems and formally put forward the startling idea of a City Manager for Allentown as the best solution to the problems. For a man to suggest the abandonment of the form of government he had so proudly instituted through the creation of the 1914 City Charter, which he had always identified as one of his principal accomplishments, was symptomatic of his virtual despair with the City Council's obstructionism. Mal still went on as though encouraging himself and stated that, most of all, the mayor "must be able to take it." He explained that he was referring to the political and social strains of the job. One example was the five banquets he once attended in a single night. He must have also meant the criticism he endured from the Council following his demands for action on city projects. The strain of office was obviously telling in his words, ever more gaunt faced, and tightly buttoned coat which now appeared on all his public photos. Nevertheless, he advised that "there is only one way to get things done and that is to hammer away, keep hammering, hammering." Even with the last effort he made on the city needs, he concluded that he would consider himself lucky to realize, when his term was up, even ten percent of his civic dreams of 1919. For this failure he blamed the "selfish and conflicting interests of others that gnaw away at different parts of [my] goals until they practically disappear into nothingness."

When speaking to the Torch Club on November 10, Mal expanded on his theme of the need for major change in city government. He again suggested dismantling the Mayor-Council Charter and replacing it with a City Manager system. Mal returned to his old theme of economy, claiming that the city could save $100,000 per year with a city manager. Its government would then be run by an outside non-partisan professional.

Nevertheless, Mal kept trying. In his last year in office, he continued promoting federal programs as a solution to the city's problems. When he took office in 1936, Mal identified housing as a major city problem. He pointed out that home ownership in the city had fallen disastrously from 75 percent to 40 percent during the Depression. Mal's solution was federal funds to support the Housing Authority. In a major statement at the end of 1939 he praised Hanover Acres, which the Authority built, as the first successful public housing project in the state. He pointed to the jobs created by the project and the money saved by eliminating slums which bred disease and crime, ultimately costing the city money. Mal saw Hanover Acres as giving people a chance to control their own living spaces again, plus a chance to change their lives and outlooks. Mal was unafraid of federal programs somehow intruding on the city's prerogatives. He saw housing and jobs as what Allentown needed, and Hanover Acres provided both, notwithstanding that Washington was the source of the funding.

Earlier in 1938, Charlie Ettinger, whom Mal had rewarded for his support with an appointment to the Housing Authority, had in his newspaper column praised Mal's long hours, hard days, and promptness as mayor. Whether this article was a trial balloon for a fifth term in 1940 or an answer to criticism that Mal was no longer attending evening events, it failed to push Mal into one more run for office. Instead, in September of 1938, Mal announced that he would not accept another nomination for mayor. Mal declared himself an "old man now" (age 66) in a news release.

Mal's last year in office saw him still putting forth his favorite programs for the city. Newspaper photos show him at various official functions designed to promote Allentown, such as the opening of "Friendship House" by the Chamber of Commerce. He also began a last major publicity campaign to make the public aware of the park system, speaking on the parks at every opportunity and writing newspaper articles about them.

Mal also promoted the Allentown Flower Show which had been started several years earlier by the Women's Club. He was responsible for having roses from his beloved Rose Garden (later named in his honor) displayed at the show for the first time. He also arranged for his wife Mabel (in her first public photo in three years) to appear with Mrs. Stanley Howe, the featured guest at the show and wife of the executive secretary to Mayor LaGuardia of New York City. As a result, the flower show had its most notable success and featured the Rose Garden, which drew the attention Mal wanted for the park system.

On a more tangible level, Mal managed to arrange for a swap with the federal government of the old post office building at 6th and Turner Streets for city land at 5th and Hamilton. Mal's plan was that the old post office would become a new city hall.

The newspapers called his transaction "the biggest real estate bargain in history." Though, as so often in the past, the Council failed to cooperate. They refused to appropriate the $50,000 necessary to convert the post office building, possibly because the WPA was, again, a necessary partner. It took another two decades until his son, Jack, as mayor, was able to erect a new city hall at 4th and Hamilton Streets.

Mal also played a major role in promoting the new Allentown-Bethlehem Airport. He saw the airport as having two significant attractions. First, it provided an important opportunity for cooperation with Bethlehem. Mal believed strongly in a regional approach to government and had been active in the Tri-City League with officials of both Bethlehem and Easton, so an airport operated with Bethlehem was a natural expansion of the regional theme. Second, a modern airport was critical to modern cities. United Airlines, however, would not continue using the new airport without adequate lighting and proper radio equipment. As a result, the whole project was in danger. The federal government was willing to supply $60,000 worth of radio equipment but only if Allentown and Bethlehem paid for the lighting.

Mal wanted the city to spend its share of the money, but the City Council balked and first asked private sources to find the funds. Its members even refused to attend meetings on the subject. When no private support could be found, Mal orchestrated public pressure on the council: four service clubs and the Chamber of Commerce petitioned the council to spend the funds. Editorials supported the idea. Mal had been able to form new alliances to promote his city projects even as his term neared its end.

The council still voted against it. On December 7, 1937, after meeting privately with the council as a committee of the whole, Mal was able to push through the authority for him to spend up to $10,000 on the lighting if Bethlehem did the same. Working quietly, Mal had managed to keep the airport project moving ahead, using his old techniques of publicity, constant pressure, and support from influential citizens, regardless of party.

The problems in Europe and Asia had begun to intrude into city affairs almost from the start of Mal's last term. Mal hoped that the United States would avoid military involvement abroad, probably because as a member of the draft board in World War I, he had come to know the responsibility of sending young men to a foreign war. In 1936, on Memorial Day, Mal tried to use that national day to call for a "calm greatly needed in these times of anxiety abroad." And, in 1939, Mal wrote to support the "Into the Synagogue" movement at Allentown's Temple Beth-El, that, "religion was the only solution of the troubles which beset us on every side." As mayor, he officially denounced the use of the American flag as a cover for Nazism, Fascism, and Communism. Mal hoped, in this way, to help avoid America becoming entangled with the various foreign ideologies which, in Europe, were accelerating the drift into war.

When war actually came, and in 1940, included a Soviet attack on Finland, Mal was asked to head the local chapter of the Finnish relief organization and to raise money for victims of Soviet oppression. He accepted and when telephoned at City Hall, made a surprisingly blunt and angry statement:

> I am for peace and have always held that we should keep our nose out of European affairs, but every time I read about what is happening to the courageous Finns, I feel like taking a gun and fighting.

First, the Depression had drained Allentown's prosperity. Next, the political failure of the city's form of government had blocked a pragmatic acceptance of potentially helpful New Deal programs. Now, a World War in which the powerful would prey on the weak and Allentown boys would be sent to fight and die was about to claim the national government's total attention. After four years of "hammering away" for progress in Allentown, Mal let his emotions show in defense of "little Finland."

Mal's official statement was somewhat more tempered, but still opened with, "[B]itterly do American citizens feel the invasion of a sister republic." He made clear that, despite his uncharacteristic emotion on the issue, he lacked the energy for a personal canvass for funds. The drive eventually raised $437.01, mostly from local churches. Mal proudly noted, shortly after he left office in 1940, that the response was from the city's "heart."

On January 2, 1940, Mal swore in his successor, George Erich. This time, editorials and letters from his fellow mayors around the state (apparently organized by Ettinger) praised him and his work. One news writer wrote: "[In] the decades [that] saw the city's greatest progress ... [it] is no mere coincidence that such advancement came during a period of almost uninterrupted leadership by one man ..."Another newspaper noted the "kindly smile" (which its photographer rarely caught) and praised his "vision" even in the face of severe criticism which "cut deep ... he never wavered from his goal." The Chamber of Commerce passed a resolution in his honor. A testimonial dinner was scheduled at the Americus Hotel featuring his friend Stanley Home of New York, his successor Mayor Erich, and the president of the League of Third Class Cities. Mal must have felt that, at least by the end of his fourth term, the city appreciated his efforts, and he could not fail to remember the contrast with the end of his third term when he was virtually ignored. At last, he had been vindicated in his efforts and beliefs.

On January 1, 2, and 3, 1940, as Mal was leaving office, the *Evening Chronicle* ran a three-part series of interviews with him. These three newspaper pieces form the most lengthy and candid record of Mal's background and philosophy. The stories first detail the incredible growth of Allentown during his term as city solicitor and four-term mayor. The Eighth Street Bridge, the parks, the sewage disposal system, the incinerator plant, and the Tilghman Street Bridge are mentioned in the stories, but not by Mal. Instead, the writer notes these things, and Mal modestly says, "I merely did a job I was getting paid to do." Mal had thought out carefully the image he wished to leave with the public, which was that of a quiet, faithful public servant who had co-written the city's charter, and then, "remaining in the background" pushed through a host of municipal improvements.

Mal took credit for the park system. He did so because he felt it was not yet established in the public eye as vital to the city. Critics are quoted as saying, "[A] he thinks about is parks," which some had called "Gross's Folly." "Nevertheless, in support of the parks, Mal first pointed out Allentown's other strengths such as its location, tax rate, sewer, water, fire, and police services, which were as good as those of any other city in America. He then argued that the city's parks system was its "ace in the hole" because "no other city can touch it."

Mal speculated that Allentown was able to attract industry (i.e., jobs) with its "ace" and was certain that, at a minimum, the parks provided the citizens with heartfelt, outdoor recreation and relaxation. He attributed the large, well-developed park system to the careful professional approach used by the city in planning it, the powerful interest of General Trexler, and the federal WPA program. Thus, he marshaled his arguments for a civic project carefully, gave credit to others, and then used the project's success to demonstrate the importance of a professional approach to government.

Mal offered the opinion that only during his most recent term had the city finally realized the beauty of what had been created. He attributed this new acceptance of the value of the parks to the success of the rose garden and chrysanthemum show at Trexler Park. Modestly, he failed to mention his own publicity campaign during the last year which had featured news stories about a tour of the parks by the mayor to draw attention to their value.

In his final interview, Mal also spoke of the future. Perhaps recognizing that jobs remained the first priority for a city racked by years of Depression, Mal called for "the development of a planned program of industrial expansion." As always, he supported government action, but only if it was planned and professional. Mal didn't fear government, only those who abused its power. Mal hoped to use government for city progress with professional direction to avoid a spoils system.

It is not surprising that Mal put the need for economic development as the top priority for the city's future, or that he wanted the efforts in that regard to be "planned" (i.e., professional), not political. These were ideas compelled by the hard times tempered with his long-held views. Mal then added his own hope that the industrial development could be accomplished by encouraging and developing the "many small struggling manufacturing concerns" already in the city. A good sport, Mal opposed the "theft" of business from another city. That was a forlorn hope and is best shown by the "industrial development" brought from other towns that his son Jack's administration claimed as one of its prime achievements in the 60s.

Mal's second recommendation for the future was some type of "showmanship," which would bring the city national fame. He argued that the city needed some new way to call attention to itself. He disclosed that at one point he and other unnamed "city fathers" had considered dropping the name "town" from the city's name. One can only speculate when that discussion about renaming the city "Allen" took place, but it likely involved General Trexler and others who saw the city as a thing of vast hope and potential. The cast of characters around Mal by 1940 lacked that kind of optimism. Mal's idea was to draw national attention to the city by making a dramatic statement that the town had become something more. The fact that Mal wanted stunts for the city showed that his appreciation of the need for drama was part of his perceived role as mayor. Drama, always dignified, of course, brought positive attention to a city and raised morale. Mal saw the need for an intangible civic pride as also at the core of a successful city government.

Although Mal's advice for the city's future promotion may have been quixotic, as with his earlier proposal of city manager, he apparently felt the need to stimulate ideas for solving the city's huge problems at the end of a Depression and beginning of a war. This mix of grand ideas implemented by specific proposals, which Mal then relentlessly followed up, was Mal's great strength. Mal also clearly knew where the city's population growth was headed "west," he said, pointing to the potential for College Heights, which had been annexed during his third term. Mal knew where Allentown was going and had given serious thought to what vehicle could best take it there even if he was no longer its driving force.

Jack's Five Years

The phone in my apartment in Berwyn, PA was in the hall passageway. The apartment was good sized (that and being cheap were its only advantages,) so the phone bell was turned up full force. The sound of that bell before dawn was like a series of shrieks. I groped from the bedroom already knowing, not sensing, knowing, something was terribly wrong at home in Allentown. Uncle Francis "Fritz" Lieberman, our family doctor, spoke, "Mal, your father has just died of a heart attack. Your mother wants to speak to you."

It was September 5, 1964, and Allentown's Camelot, like the nation's, was over. Or almost! There was still the funeral, the letters, telegrams and phone calls of condolence and sadness—no, true shock and real grief that such a force was gone. The last five years had been like sudden riches. John T. ("Jack") Gross began his second term as mayor with enthusiasm and confidence seemingly everywhere—only nine months before his death. Malcolm W. "Mal," Jack's father, had grown slowly into the gigantic figure symbolizing Allentown in the 1920s, and then, Atlas-like, sustaining the glimmer of a vision of the future in the bleakness of the 1930s. Jack Gross had burst on the Allentown political scene in 1959.

Jack's connection to Allentown throughout his adult life had been much more tenuous than his father's. The dark economic times of Mal's last term had forced Jack out of Muhlenberg College after his junior year. A job at Pennsylvania Power & Light Company was more important than a college degree. PP&L eventually sent him to New York City. Later, he lived in Harrisburg, with his wife Agnes, as Deputy Secretary of Commerce in Democratic Governor George Leader's administration. At least six inches shorter, at 5'10" (he added a "half" when asked his height), than Mal, he somehow looked taller. Perhaps it was his slim figure, dark good looks and New York-cut suits.

Even when he was in Harrisburg, he and Agnes had maintained a home in Allentown at 115$^{1/2}$ North 17th Street and returned there virtually every weekend. During those weekends, he continued his social and business contacts in the city, particularly at the popular local Elks Club. Politics was not part of these activities. Jack considered being a candidate for Allentown School Board, probably in 1939 or 1941, but Mal had brutally forbidden it.

Otherwise, he stayed clear of local elections and even voted Republican in 1940. His health was also a problem. Almost from his birth on March 5, 1909, his childhood had been filled with a series of life-threatening illnesses that continued to plague him as an adult. Lockjaw almost killed him after he stepped on a rusty nail. Empyema (a lung abscess) had cost him a rib from an emergency surgery that Dr. Charles Schaffer performed to save his life, and a ruptured appendix resulted in another life-and-death operation. Then, a strange wasting illness put him in Allentown Hospital for months, again near death. Only a pony purchased by Mal as a last resort and shown to him through the hospital window finally made him rally.

As was often the case in the late nineteenth and early twentieth centuries, a family doctor suggested a more "healthy" climate. As a result, his mother Mabel, younger sister Betty and Jack moved to Southern California to live with his grandmother, Nevilla Yost. There he dominated the western boys at basketball, a new game in California, which was already popular in the East. Perhaps his repeated brushes with death made him a daredevil. When he returned to Allentown, Jack was expelled from Allentown High School for setting off firecrackers in the boys' locker room. He smoked cigarettes at the local pool halls, eventually getting a three-pack-a-day habit. He finally graduated from Allentown Preparatory School, now Muhlenberg's West Hall. His academic career at Muhlenberg was hardly stellar, but he came to deeply love his college and his fraternity, A.T.O.

After leaving Muhlenberg, Mal tried to land him a job with Franklin Roosevelt's New Deal in Washington. Despite managing to get Jack an appointment with FDR's legendary Postmaster General Jim Farley, no patronage position was offered. Finally, he found a job in PP&L's "loop course" and eventually worked for the power company until the mid-1950s.

In September 1957, he purchased the Woefoel Pretzel Bakery at 13th and Union Streets and returned to Allentown full time. About the same time, he bought controlling interest in Grandview Cemetery Association on Walbert Avenue in South Whitehall Township. Neither offered him the challenge that he now almost obsessively pursued. He quickly lost interest in both businesses as he had earlier schemes for an ice-skating rink and for turning Lehigh County into a supplier of tomatoes for Campbell's soup.

In the late 1950s Allentown was no longer the rapidly expanding city of Mal's years. Instead, it was a mature urban community based on truck manufacturing at Mack Trucks on its South Side, an upscale residential neighborhood in the West End, with retail business as its heart, centered downtown at Hess Bros. Department Store at 9th and Hamilton Streets. Its blue-collar workers lived in row houses, its business and professional elite in single-family ranchers and fake Tudors.

Allentown's government was still based on a city charter written by Mal as city solicitor in 1915. That charter gave the mayor an important title, but minimum power. The mayor had only one vote of five on the council, which controlled all city affairs.

Despite a Republican majority in Allentown for many of the years the new charter was in effect, Democrats had managed to win seven of nine elections for mayor. This was partly because Mal himself had won four of those Democratic victories, and also because city and Lehigh County voters had a peculiar tendency to allot particular offices to each party. The four Allentown City Council seats did not follow this pattern, but instead, tended to be hotly contested with varying results and shifting majorities often every two years. The result, as Mal found out in his last term (1936-1940), was a great challenge for the mayor. As the perceived head of local government, he was expected to act as a true executive. Yet the shifting sands of council votes on which the mayor was required to stand made any coherent and consistent program impossible. To make matters worse, the local Democratic Party, faction-ridden and unable to control the votes of its own council members, was generally no match for the better-disciplined Republicans.

These political inconsistencies may have explained why no mayor since Mal in 1927 had been elected to a second consecutive term. In 1958, when Jack and his family settled back in town, Democrat Donald V. Hock was mayor with a Democratic majority on council. Hock had won, lost, and won again as mayor. A professional toastmaster, attorney and author, he had brought certain panache to the office. Small and trim, Hock had a confident swagger about him. Nevertheless, his constant, well-publicized travels and private law practice created an undercurrent of discontent. Allentonians had a sense that the city was slowly decaying, that the mayor was not always on the job, and that the wave of post-war activity in other cities was missing in the Queen City. In Allentown there was a malaise.

Jack, back in town and already restless in the pretzel business, was a natural magnet for these discontents. Nearing 50, his hair still jet black, his larger-than-life father dead 15 years, he must have felt that his time, at last, had come. Throughout 1958, Jack considered a race for mayor, frustrated at times by the divided leadership in the Democratic Party, but gradually assembling a group who would lead his campaign against Mayor Hock. Eventually, with his brother-in-law, attorney Ray Brennen, as de facto campaign manager, and businessman Harry Harley as his principal fund raiser, together with Edward F. Rabenold (later vice-president of Chrysler First), he moved against the incumbent.

Allentown is nearly the same size today as in 1959. However, its elections are notably different. The city's ethnic mix was far less complex, and was primarily made up of Pennsylvania Dutch with a significant Irish and less-numerous Jewish Eastern European and Italian minorities. Jack's Elks Club was one of innumerable clubs, societies, labor unions, church groups and similar institutions of long standing which were the subtle threads holding the political structure together.

These clubs, lodges and unions had brought the city's people through the worst twenty years in America's history, a decade of Depression and a decade of real and cold wars. They formed the cells of the community within the city, and office seekers needed their support to win. "Political" issues tended to be matters that affected their group as a whole, not their members as individuals. Neighborhoods were real as well. The "Ward," the "West End," the "East Side" and "Mountainville" were identifiable and distinct with their own "issues" about garbage pickup, street cleaning, and illegal parking. Formal neighborhood associations were unnecessary— people saw each other over their backyard fences, on their front porches and in the alleys, which formed the rear grid of passageways in every block. A tremendous amount of civic pride was also present about Allentown as a city. Mal and the city fathers of the 20s had created the myth of Allentown as a great metropolis. That myth, confirmed by the reality of the grand parks, shopping district and manufacturing section, was important to the people who lived here. Allentown was the unrivaled center of Lehigh County. And Jack, with his family name from the past and connections to the future in the state and nation, symbolized what the city's people thought they needed to recapture their past and gain their future.

In the late 1950s, little was heard or reported about a political contest after the candidates formally announced. *The Morning Call* and *Evening Chronicle* did not cover Jack's campaign at all after he announced his candidacy; they covered only Hock's actions as mayor. Personal contact with the influential individuals at each small club or lodge, window signs in corner grocery stores and banquets were the stuff of a successful campaign. Jack, of course, had the loyal support of his father's still worshipful followers led by Charlie Ettinger, *The Call's* Harrisburg reporter and deputy head of Allentown Housing Authority. He also made the nightly circuit of clubs and fire halls where there was also a good deal of buying of rounds by the candidate.

"Clean campaigns" —meaning issue-less campaigns—were in vogue. Jack did emphasize that he would be a full-time mayor, playing to Hock's weakness of too many outside activities. Jack also had one secret weapon as well, the U.S. mail. For the first time locally, all registered Democrats were mailed a colorful brochure asking for their vote and emphasizing Jack's impressive credentials. This was Ray Brennen's key to victory. The two Democratic County Committee people in each of the city's 50-odd precincts also got a free can of Gross Pretzels plus cocktails and dinner at the Elks Club. News reporters got a dinner as well, but no pretzels. Polling was unknown at the local level, but Robert Beam (later a South Whitehall Township commissioner) took his own poll at 9th and Hamilton Streets by simply asking passersby how they intended to vote. It came out dead even. Large newspaper ads in the last week of the campaign were also a staple and were read and commented on throughout the town, much like the Super Bowl ads of today.

It all worked. Jack defeated Hock in the primary by approximately 3,000 votes (a two-to-one margin). As a result, he faced Ezra "Jack" Fetzer, who defeated former Mayor Brighton C.

Diefenderfer for the Republican nomination. Both parties' voters had clearly signaled that they wanted something different. For tradition-bound Allentown this promised to be significant.

Jack's fall campaign again stressed his "experience" with PP&L and the state. This was intended to contrast him with Fetter, a door-to-door salesman, but avoid a charge of "dirty campaigning." The "real" meaning of the political message was then spread by word of mouth through the clubs and union halls where the code words of the public campaign were explained. A much nastier word-of-mouth campaign came from the Republican side with a rumor that Jack was a secret Roman Catholic. His wife was actually a practicing Catholic, but Jack remained a nominal Lutheran. Jack failed in efforts to recruit Reverend Henry Pflum, pastor of Christ Lutheran Church, for his campaign committee so as to not-so-subtly rebut the rumor.

In every speech, Jack unashamedly mentioned Mal, and he formed a bipartisan committee headed by Harley and his old friend from the Elks, Republican attorney Charles G. Helwig. Political committees were a feature of every campaign. Allentonians loved reading the list of names, carefully balanced (when the campaign was really well connected) by ethnic, occupational and political considerations.

Jack was able to present himself as someone who came from the glorious past, yet someone who could bring Allentown into the national and state flow of events with his experience and bipartisan support. He was both safe and new at the same time, a rare advantage for a politician.

The Democratic State Committee gave Jack no financial support, but did send one of its operatives to Allentown, who used the curious method of riding in as many taxicabs as possible in a single day and questioning the cabbies about the upcoming election. He reported that this informal poll resulted in a prediction of an easy win for Jack, but otherwise a Republican sweep.

The taxi poll proved accurate. Jack almost coasted to a 4,000-vote victory. However, the Republicans won virtually every other county and city office and regained a three-to-two majority on council.

Realizing his need to stitch together enough council votes for the major programs he hoped to pursue, Jack immediately reached out to new Republican Councilman Richard Snyder for support. Snyder, surprised by this unusual break in party ranks, quickly formed a personal and political friendship with Jack. Eventually, Jack formed a similar bond with Republican Councilman Samuel Fenstermacher.

At the same time, Jack began contacts with I. Cyrus "Cy" Gutman, who headed the Industrial Development Authority, Albert "Bert" Bickel from the Housing Authority and Philip "Phil" I. Berman, whom he planned to make head of the Redevelopment Authority. Each was flattered by the mayor-elect's personal interest and energized to move their heretofore-inert boards in step with Jack's plans for government activity. Like Mal, Jack looked to the mayor's power in appointing authority members and then using those bodies to move major projects as a way around roadblocks on council.

The one city department the mayor automatically headed, police, was of no interest to him, and was a political liability. Jack had a secret survey of the department by the Pennsylvania State Police that evaluated its officers' honesty and connections to organized crime. As a result, following his father's example in 1937, Jack quickly selected as the new chief Walter C. Wickert, an Army veteran, with Gerald Monahan Sr. as chief of detectives. Deferring to his new appointees' commendations, Jack cut back on the number of department "brass" by demoting the former chief and other ranking officers to patrolmen. Jack claimed his reorganization would save $17,000 and be more efficient. Mal had invariably used the same themes to support changes in his administration. In both cases, they also formed a convenient cover for demoting political opponents. Even with police civil service, there were still ways to punish Hock supporters in the police department and reorganization was the most effective.

Jack used similar logic to justify a reduction in the law department staff by eliminating a secretary to save another $4,000. Both moves drew some criticism in the press about the loss of valuable experienced city personnel, but they also sent a message that Jack was now in charge of the Democratic Party in City Hall. Police politics were trouble for a mayor, and Jack sought to avoid them by deferring to the "professionals" running the department.

In a wide-ranging interview at the *Call-Chronicle* on November 8, Jack discussed his experiences in his first political campaign. It had obviously been a revelation to one who had not come up through the political ranks of alderman or school director as had most of his colleagues. Two things made an impression on him.

First was the awesome power of his father's name. "I am a very fortunate individual," he said, referring to his father's still-revered name. The power of that name nearly 20 years after Mal left office says much about the stability of Allentown's population as late as 1959. Though much had changed in the world, the same voters and their children lived here and still remembered Mal.

Next, Jack noted the voters' concern for more than the tiresome controversies over whether Linden Street should be one-way and moving the Center Square monument. The campaign taught him the importance of the city's neighborhoods on the South and East sides. Nevertheless, the preservation of the downtown shopping district had also come to be a top priority even if it meant destroying the center-city neighborhoods around it. This paradox was to have far-reaching consequences for the city's neighborhoods and communities who elected him.

Finally, Jack admitted that the campaign experience had been "a little frightening." His name and new ideas raised people's expectations, and he warned that he was not up to them.

Several weeks later, speaking to the B'nai B'rith, he kept his talk to generalities, mentioning again the need for both city industrial development and redevelopment programs. He also noted two immediate crises. Mack Trucks was considering leaving town, and City Hall in the 600 block of Linden Street was "an old wreck."

On January 5, 1960, Jack and Republican Dick Snyder, the other newcomer to council, were sworn in along with veteran Republican Lloyd E. Grammes who continued in charge of the patronage-laden Street Department. Jack made a brief general speech and was photographed smiling with "First Lady" Agnes.

Jack's first action was to insist that council meet on time. In the era before Sunshine Laws required all official business to be transacted in public, council had fallen into the habit of having long closed sessions in the mayor's office before the "official" public meeting. It was during those sessions that the horse-trading for each council member's pet project took place while the public waited outside for the rubber stamp at the public meeting. No one seemed to mind the secrecy, but the wait annoyed them, according to local news reports.

Jack's promptness was warmly praised in the press and set a tone of a new efficiency in city government. It also sent a message that the mayor had taken charge.

Jack next moved to more substantive problems, and specifically, Mack Trucks' possible move to Hagerstown, Maryland. His approach, which was to become typical, was to mobilize local support and then network to his powerful state and federal government contacts to identify which of Mack's specific needs each could solve. Jack brought Democratic Governor David Lawrence into a series of personal meetings with Mack officials. Out of those meetings came concerns for the cost of its current union contract. Jack then brought Lawrence into talks with United Auto Workersofficials with the result, that the union agreed to roll back its most recent wage increase.

Learning that Mack needed a new location, Jack obtained commitments for local financing and federal and state assistance. He was even able to get federal authorities to release government land on the south side near Convair Air Field (now Queen City Airport) for a new Mack plant if necessary. Although Mack decided not to use property around Convair, Jack did not forget that land for possible other new industries.

Eventually, Mack announced only a partial victory for Jack. It would not close the Allentown plant, but neither would it consolidate all of its operations in the city. The union felt cheated, and intense new contract talks began which finally resulted in a contract protecting senior workers, but putting those hired since 1955 at risk for layoff. Not surprisingly, the younger workers reacted angrily to the proposed contract. Jack became personally and publicly involved as he pleaded for ratification to at least save the Allentown plant. His plea and the tight leadership control of the union succeeded when a majority of the workers voted for the contract on July 31, 1960, after a contentious meeting at Allentown High's Little Palestra.

Jack's efforts showed the dramatic change in Allentown's power centers since Mal's day. Big business with its base in New York faced big labor based in Detroit. To match this now-national power,

Jack's ties to the governor in Harrisburg were vital. And Jack knew how to use those ties.

Mack was saved as Allentown's major industry, and over the next two decades the city would become its "World Headquarters." Nevertheless, the residue of labor-management bitterness as the "55'ers" came to power in the union eventually would cause the company to leave Allentown for South Carolina. That was all in the distant future. Mack with its thousands of highly paid blue-collar workers was safe, and Jack could move to jump-starting the City Redevelopment Plan.

Redevelopment was essentially massed capital from federal, state and local government to purchase, tear down and open up for new construction sections of cities that were viewed as "blighted." Once this was accomplished, with construction of government buildings leading the way, the cleared area was rebuilt, based on what was thought to be rational city planning. New apartments, town houses and hotels were to be featured around the government buildings.

In Allentown, that meant two million dollars in federal grants, further generous federal loans, more than $500,000 of state money and $640,000 of city cash and services. Using a redevelopment authority that Jack appointed and constantly spurred forward, these funds bought 20 acres of properties in the area southeast of Fifth and Hamilton Streets. Directly tied to this action was a city commitment to a huge new City Hall in the area.

After years of inactivity, the speed of redevelopment in Jack's first year was truly blinding. He did it with constant pressure and flattery centered on the Allentown business community. Its leaders, including department store executive John Henry Leh, attorney Morris Efron and banker Frank Cressman, were honored, prodded by and photographed with the mayor. Jack had quickly come to realize that his ability to achieve results was based on the prestige of his title, his family name and his superior knowledge of how redevelopment programs worked. His national and state contacts were also crucial to get Allentown to the front of the line for federal and state money. Jack's appearance of power was much greater than his actual authority. He still had only one vote on council. However, he had the title of mayor and the last name of

Gross, and that meant something in a city and county where no other political official had any similar rank. Jack quickly came to know how to use that appearance of power.

Ironically, Jack's major adversary was Democratic Councilman Bill "Bull" Ritter. Ritter's department in the city was the Finance Bureau, which permitted him to manipulate and control council's actions and plans by simply announcing that the city lacked the money for a project. Since city government had to operate with a balanced budget, no money meant no action was possible. A large man with a bald head topping a moonlike face framed with huge glasses, Ritter had a reputation as a fiscal watchdog. From the beginning of Jack's term, Ritter proved difficult. Only two days after he took office, Jack was confronted with a demand from city employees for a raise. Since the budget for 1960 was already barely in balance, the new administration either had to turn down the demand and face labor unrest or hike taxes for the raise. Then, over $116,000 was "discovered," which Ritter as finance director had held back from 1959 tax receipts. Confronted on the issue, Ritter claimed he "did not have the time to process" the money. As a result, council was able to vote a $200 yearly pay raise for city workers.

In April 1960, Ritter again caused Jack problems with council. Under Allentown's system of government, the street-lighting program was part of the mayor's budget. But that budget was short $7,500 for 1960, and Ritter fought Jack's efforts to have it increased. Jack threatened no new streetlights in Allentown without the money, which, he argued, was "needed now." He bitterly attacked Ritter for sending an employee to a convention while the street-lighting money was being held up. Jack prevailed, again, but his public anger was reflective of his frustration with management by committee, made necessary by Allentown's form of government. More significantly, Jack lacked the patience and interest to play the political games of that system, especially over streetlights and convention expenses. Allentown politics has long favored contrarians like Ritter, but Ritter's constant negatives and roadblocks infuriated Jack, who simply couldn't deal with delay.

Jack's political problems were compounded by his arrest for speeding going to Harrisburg. The arrest drew statewide publicity. Nevertheless, he turned the embarrassment to his advantage by quickly accepting a 15-day driving suspension and got praise from *The Morning Call* for taking his punishment. Ritter and a speeding ticket were not going to slow him down.

A party political struggle on council over appointments of the city solicitor, his assistants and the city clerk also erupted. Jack hoped to save at least one of the current Democratic lawyers in the solicitor's office. He failed when, by a straight party vote of 3 to 2, council named three Republicans to the positions.

A less straightforward battle took place over City Clerk George Kistler's reappointment. Although a Democrat, Kistler was unpopular in party circles, and Jack refused to re-nominate him. Jack's maneuver blocked the appointment, because given local political protocol, Kistler's Republican council supporters couldn't move his nomination. Ritter, council's other Democrat, finally did so, and Jack voted with the other council members for Kistler with the cryptic statement that, "I felt this action should be unanimous."

National politics also briefly intruded onto the city scene. Another Jack, Jack Kennedy, was running his now-legendary campaign to become the first Catholic president. Kennedy was not Jack Gross' choice. He actually tried to lead a brief, pathetic boomlet for Chester Bowles, former congressman and ambassador to India, and was embarrassed when he accidentally wrote in Bowles name for another office, not President, in the Democratic primary. Jack Gross was much more at home with the big business/big labor faction of the party. Bowles, Adlai Stevenson or later Lyndon Johnson (New Deal, not New Frontier Democrats) made him much more comfortable. And he had no interest in the national economic or international issues of the day. Jack loyally introduced Kennedy to the massive crowd of 80,000 to 100,000 that packed Center Square for a spectacular Kennedy visit.

If anything Kennedy said impressed him, Jack, and Agnes too, failed to note it. Instead, his only comments were surprise that Kennedy was rather short and wore lifts under his shoes to make him look taller. (Could these actually have been some form of support of the future president's bad back?)

The massive Kennedy crowd did impress Jack. It was the first sign of the pride and sense of importance Allentown's citizens were again beginning to feel after the long decades of Depression and war.

The "people," as Jack began referring to Allentonians, were starting to see themselves as a unit moving toward the goal of a great new city. The idea of the people being Allentown as a collective whole began to take shape in Jack's statements. Naturally, he also began to see himself as the voice of that whole.

Then came the results of the 1960 census, which initially recorded a drop in the city's population by two percent to 104,000. City population was viewed as a vital sign of civic health, and the announcement of a decline caused a major Allentown morale problem. Population growth was about more than taxes and voting power. It was a key measure of whether a city was living or dying. It was also becoming an obsession of Jack's. He gloomily noted that the drop confirmed, "that many of our people are continuing to move to suburban areas." Earlier, he had tried to meet this trend by quietly trying to annex a portion of South Whitehall Township, which formed an "island" surrounded by Allentown's West End. The effort had been a miserable failure. People living in the suburbs did not want to live in Allentown, which was now permanently locked into the boundaries set by Mal's earlier annexations. As suburban population growth and city decline continued, the political leadership of the entire county, which had previously been funneled to the city mayor's office, became more and more fragmented.

In late May, a recheck of the census figures showed Allentown had actually gained population to over 108,000, passing Reading, to become the state's fifth-largest city. Civic pride was temporarily revived, but Jack knew that the long-range picture for city population growth remained dark, and he never came to recognize that a declining city population might actually be an advantage if its quality were maintained. As a result, he left as part of his legacy a need for population growth at all costs. In an effort to fulfill that legacy, city policy in the next twenty years encouraged conversion of homes to apartments to sustain the impression of population growth even at the expense of breaking up the community that had made up that population.

For now, Allentown was relieved to be one of the state's few cities that was still able to advertise its growth, but real population growth for Allentown was over after 1960, regardless of the new census figures, and Jack knew it. If it was to survive, Allentown had to reinvent itself within the walls the suburbs had politically put up around it.

Still, for now, confidence was high, so high that in November, when PP&L announced it was moving from 9th and Hamilton to the suburbs, no particular concern was voiced by the city's officials. Nothing like the effort to save Mack Trucks occurred. Instead, Jack secretly planned to lure the recently announced Lehigh County Community College into the PP&L building to create a tower of learning like the University of Pittsburgh, and Max Hess, the flamboyant owner of Hess's, immediately offered two and one-half million dollars for the city's tallest building.

PP&L eventually decided to remain downtown; however, the lack of concern about its possible leaving is significant. Allentown was staking its all on retail shopping. Commercial office buildings in the downtown were no longer to be a priority. Neighborhoods in center city were to be sacrificed to retail shopping. Even the upper stories of Hamilton Street stores were allowed to decay. The value of the first-floor retail space would carry "The Street" by itself. Jack was committed to maintaining "The Street" at all costs.

The "Golden Acres," the Hamilton Street area roughly from Fifth to Tenth, which made up "The Street," was by 1960 the magnet for shoppers from the entire county and beyond. Jack made a campaign issue against Hock of the number of vacancies in storefronts on Hamilton Street.

Though "The Street," centered on Hess's, was booming again in the early 1960s as his first term began, a tiny dark cloud appeared to the north on MacArthur Road in Whitehall Township. Two Guys From Harrison opened a discount store only a short distance from the city, and it was open Sundays.

In retrospect, it is hard to understand why the state's "Blue Laws" barring Sunday sales were the smoke screen for the struggle, which ultimately saw Allentown's downtown destroyed. Hess's decline, parking problems and easy access were the real keys to why shoppers ultimately left Allentown. Jack tried to stem the tide with a master traffic plan for more one-way streets, parking meters and brighter streetlights. Allentown residents instinctively disliked one-way streets and parking meters. They may have sensed that parking meters and one-way streets for fast traffic killed neighborhoods. Those neighborhoods were as much the stuff of Allentown as Hess's, but no one saw that in 1960. Instead, the glitter of the "Golden Acres" distracted everyone, including Jack.

Meanwhile, the escalating side show over Two Guys continued with Jack demanding that new Republican District Attorney George Joseph enforce the Blue Laws. Joseph countered that he was a prosecutor, not a policeman. Joseph also cleverly put Jack on the defensive by pointing out Blue Laws violations in Allentown itself.

Despite all the controversy and fierce opposition from the Protestant clergy, Two Guys stayed open Sundays. Only Max Hess's public commitment to high quality and low prices at his downtown store, and his quiet purchase of Braden Baseball Field on Seventh Street to foreclose, temporarily, a possible major mall, kept "The Street" thriving. But, thrive it did during Jack's terms, with the mayor constantly appearing in the ritual news photos of new store openings and posing for more pictures with the celebrities Max Hess brought to Allentown to promote his great store.

Meanwhile, Jack also continued his efforts for industrial development. Western Electric, which ultimately became Agere, announced a major new addition to its East Side plant. Jack stressed the company's 22-million-dollar payroll and 4,200 workers when he broke ground for the new plant.

Jack's success with Western Electric was followed by more good news from Mack, which announced it was planning a million-dollar expansion. Relieved, Jack said, "This is the best news Allentown has received in many years. We now have every reason to believe our major heavy industry will stay here, and in addition, it will expand greatly."

Jack's whole industrial development plan concentrated on manufacturing jobs. Manufacturing, he believed, formed the center of a web of related support jobs. One manufacturing job created five service jobs. To accomplish this, he used an industrial development authority, which made low interest loans available to new or expanding industry.

In July came another success when Downyflake Foods announced it would build a plant in the industrial site, which Jack had created around what had been renamed Queen City Airport. Again, using the re-energized industrial development authority and state funding through the Pennsylvania Industrial Development Authority, Jack orchestrated new industry and expansion of city companies in the park. Sarco (later Spirax Sarco) soon followed with another plant as the city spent $68,000 to continue to develop the park. Jack emphasized the 500 new manufacturing jobs the city money would help generate.

The industrial park was born. The land around Queen City Airport was virtually the last space available for the type of sites demanded by the new concept. Suburban areas, with their large tracts of already cleared farmland, had plenty of such sites, and developers eventually found them. Ironically, Jack's industrial park set an example that ultimately attracted industry from the city to its suburbs.

Meanwhile, petty disputes on council continued to nag and irritate Jack. Bull Ritter constantly opposed any city spending initiatives. Jack's solution was to encourage the Allentown Jaycees to take on the project of a new home rule charter. He already made clear his preference for changing the form of government to a strong mayor; however, had he taken the lead in an effort to vote on a new charter, his relations with his Republican allies on council would have been strained. No council member wanted to admit he wasn't doing his job, or worse, to lose his job to a new form of government. Jack's solution was to hire the nonpartisan Jaycees to take the lead, with the Trojan horse of a "study commission" rather than an outright vote, on a new form of government. The study commission would then propose a strong mayor government. With this double blind of a charter study, Jack hoped to change the future structure of city government, but avoid offending his colleagues on city council at the same time. Ironically, after his death, his plan worked, and the city, in 1967, voted for a strong mayor government based, exactly as he planned, on a nonpartisan study commission's recommendation.

State politics also intruded into Jack's first term. Jack's old chief, Secretary of Commerce William R. Devlin, died October 21, 1961. Governor Lawrence offered the position to Jack who, although he declined, signaled an interest in Harrisburg by stating he had "no ambition in that direction" (i.e., a mere state cabinet post). Earlier, Jack had been mentioned in the Allentown newspapers for the office he really hoped for, governor.

The year ended with work on the new city hall well under way and a drive to put a new courthouse next to it at 5th and Hamilton started as well. Despite two strikes at Mack Trucks, which deeply worried Jack because of the jobs the company brought the city, Allentown was ready to launch itself into the new decade.

Perhaps 1961's success gave Jack the confidence to propose a new $10 "jobs" tax to permit a balanced 1962 budget and another raise for city employees late in the year. The tax was a new idea for Pennsylvania cities and gave Allentown a huge revenue boost. Suburban taxpayers hired George Joseph to fight it, and he temporarily prevailed when the Lehigh County Court declared the tax illegal. The city appealed successfully to the Pennsylvania Supreme Court, but was unable to spend the money it collected while the case was pending. The new tax seemed to promise a permanent solution to the city's yearly agony of budget balancing. And it was actually popular with city residents who had long been bitter about the suburbanites who worked here, but paid taxes elsewhere.

II

Mayor Jack Gross had never thought much of the idea of City Bicentennial celebrations, which were scheduled for 1962. Hock had made his major campaign theme in the 1959 election his change of the date on the city seal to permit the event. The existing animosity between them may have colored Jack's view of the value of a big bicentennial. And, unlike Mal, Jack never really appreciated the merit in great public events or "stunts" as Mal had called them. For Jack, hard work backed by knowledge of detail, together with a network of state and national business and political connections, were the stuff of successful city government. He never saw nor appreciated the need for a mayor to be a public cheerleader. Instead, he carried out that part of the job by endless attendance at everything going on in Allentown. He was available to cut ribbons, attend weddings or speak at union halls. His talks (not really speeches) at these events were brief, uninspiring and humorless, more like a report than an oration. His favorite position on a public platform was as master of ceremonies where he needed to make only brief "remarks" and then introduce the "real" speakers. Still, Allentonians came to consider him a "people's mayor" by his constant presence at their minor or major events. The city was small enough, and, more importantly, its inhabitants, in touch with one another because of their churches, clubs and societies as well as the actual physical closeness of its row houses, to be reachable by the pure dogged effect of showing up when asked. And so, Jack plodded on night after night to event after event, willing to put his family name with its magical connection to the city's glorious past and his title at the disposal of the city's residents.

The Bicentennial was different from this nightly grind if in no other way than by its sheer size. The final parade had 20,000 marchers with 175,000 spectators watching it for 6-1/2 hours. Significantly, at the time of the parade, Jack saved a news column about a 1928 city parade led by Mal to celebrate (prematurely) Allentown's reaching it's 100,000 population. Jack underlined the portion about his father. Was he proud to have duplicated Mal's feat, or relieved at last to have surpassed his giant father?

The Bicentennial was much more than a parade. For at least a year beforehand, Jack's allies, Edward Rabenold and Dr. Muriel Berman, carefully planned a yearlong celebration. Slowly, day-by-day, meeting-by-meeting, their committee planned a huge yearlong celebration of Allentown's power and purpose.

Included were a groundbreaking for the new City Hall by Governor Lawrence, numerous luncheons and community events and a "Brothers of the Brush" Chapter that Jack very reluctantly joined, agreeing to grow a mustache, not a full beard. Even that concession was a major sacrifice of personal standards. Jack hated beards. He considered them untidy. As a one-time New Yorker, Jack dressed flawlessly with ties, suits, socks and shirts matched and always crisp. Hair, jet black, slick with hair tonic and perfectly parted, he looked like a New York clothing store ad. That look was a political advantage in a town where other men often looked rumpled and unfashionable. Jack seemed sharp because of his sharp dress. His feet were his only problem. Any new shoes caused him blisters, which for days made him virtually unable to walk. Finally, he discovered Hanover shoes, which fit him better, and, ever after, wore only their black or brown oxfords year after year.

The Bicentennial was a success to the point that Rabenold was mentioned as a possible successor to Jack by Governor Lawrence himself. Jack had greatly underestimated the need for big public events to make the city's people feel proud to be part of a community. The huge 1960 Kennedy crowd opened his eyes. The Bicentennial made him come to know that mass public events were vital to a city in the 1960s. Commenting on the celebrations in early June, he said, "I was never prouder of Allentown than last Sunday." Jack had now come to see "the people" and "Allentown" as one powerful engine that could be relied on to move forward.

The balance of June was an afterglow of the success with more announcements on the progress of City Hall and new industry moving to the Queen City Airport site. Then on June 28, Jack had a bad night of pain. This was more than his usual coughing from his cigarettes. It was real pain, and by June 30, the public was told he had had a "mild" heart attack. Uncle Fritz Lieberman privately said it was much worse. It was "bad, very bad," but Jack refused to accept his condition. After his many previous brushes with death, he was sure his doctors could cure him. He stayed at Sacred Heart Hospital for several weeks, and cut back temporarily to six King Size Chesterfields a day, and then went to Ocean City, New Jersey, for two months of rest. The newspapers said he was in "Shangri La" and editorialized that "we're too demanding" on the mayor by asking him to work days and attend our events at night. It was a message Allentown and its mayor ignored.

By September, Jack was back at work. He refused his doctor's advice to quit smoking completely and turned a deaf ear to the pleas of a group of friends Agnes assembled to ask him to slow down. He even ignored more newspaper editorials asking the public to stop its demands on him. Instead, if anything, he increased both his day and night routine of duties.

Jack returned to work to find public housing had now started to become controversial. Mal had brought public housing to Allentown in the late 1930s to temporarily mitigate the impact of the long Depression. Hanover Acres on the East Side had been the result. Despite bitter local realtors' opposition, Jack saw a much expanded public housing program as a solution to mitigate the effects of his cherished redevelopment program. Redevelopment forced old and poor people, including many of the city's black population living in the blighted areas, to move out as their housing was torn down for new development.

Jack realized the obvious problems with tearing down the homes of the poor, black and elderly. They needed somewhere to live.

He proposed moving these dispossessed people to public housing projects. The city had a long history of major public-housing projects on its East Side but not in its blue collar, working-class neighborhoods. Residents in those neighborhoods saw public housing as moving the blight to them and responded by egging Jack's car the night before his first heart attack and setting bugs loose in his home shortly before his second. In 1963, that opposition had not yet come together, but it would in the near future.

Realtors' opposition, led by Ray Geiger Sr., was already vocal. It focused on the proposed public housing project for seniors in the north end, which ironically, after his death, would be the community's only memorial to Jack as "Gross Towers." Geiger contended the building would waste tax dollars to subsidize people who could afford to buy their own houses when they left the redevelopment areas. Jack fought the opposition realizing that if the more popular seniors' housing failed, there would be no hope for the Cumberland Gardens project on the South Side for the poor.

The continuing struggle over public housing brought out Jack's best. He bluntly, if not eloquently, argued for public housing to give people displaced by his redevelopment project a place to live. Openly supporting public housing before the Lehigh County Labor Council on October 1, 1963, he linked it with his popular redevelopment plan. "We can go no further with redevelopment until we can relocate people," he said. Ultimately, both Gross Towers and Cumberland Gardens were built, but a nasty streak of bias had shown up in Allentown in 1963, that was to widen into a gaping wound by 1964.

In truth, public housing in Allentown was never able to fulfill its promise and had serious disadvantages. Large public housing projects never really supported the fragile family structures shattered when their center-city homes were torn down. Blight hides successful family life as well as crime. Big public-housing projects were the only solution government had in the 1960s to the "people" side of decayed center cities. Jack adopted it as vital if the city were to continue to rebuild itself and decently house its poor at the same time.

Jack also quietly tried to support the minority communities who lived in the center city. He found a job with the city for the Rev. Horace Melton as relocation officer for the Redevelopment Authority, so he could continue his ministry to the black community at the same time. Jack also took up the idea of a human relations commission for the city, pushed it through council and saw his old ally, Charlie Ettinger, named its first chairman. He then appointed members, mainly clergy, who really believed in racial equality. At the same time, he warned them to be cautious and recognize that city council needed to approve the finances for its activities.

Other signs of the clash of values that was to be the hallmark of the 1960s appeared as 1963 drew to a close. A zoning application was filed in October for a coffee house by "bearded" Robert McArthur, as the *Evening Chronicle* described him. The irony of this obvious slur was apparently lost on the reporter when the whole city had been "bearded" only a year earlier for the Bicentennial. Opposition was immediate, and the mayor made clear that the city would use its inspection power to "closely watch all coffee shop proposals." Later, he secretly instructed the police to pressure coffee shops to close. This they did, forcing another coffee shop owner out of town.

World, national and state issues were further away than in Mal's last term in the 1930s. Jack loyally supported the Democratic state ticket as Democratic Senator Joseph Clark, Secretary of Internal Affairs Genevieve Blatt, and the party's gubernatorial candidate Richardson Dillworth visited Allentown in the 1962 election. His role, however, was invariably to chair the political meetings at which they spoke and little more. Only once did he inject himself personally into the election by calling Republican Congressman Willard Curtin "almost childlike" because of Curtin's attacks on his opponent, famous author James Michener. Jack and Agnes both admired Michener, who they believed was doing a great party and public service by running for office. This may have prompted Jack's then uncharacteristic partisanship on Michener's behalf.

International affairs intruded even less on the local scene. During the Cuban Missile Crisis, Jack urged residents to build fallout shelters. He spoke of the "Cuban situation being IT" and he noted, that the city must live with the threat of "bombs for a long, long time." Otherwise, the Cold War was hardly mentioned. Big local parades and Friday-night high school football games were far more important.

The Democrats lost most of the offices in the 1962 election, but as soon as the results were in, there was immediate local speculation as to the next year's Allentown mayoral race. Hock was mentioned as opposing Jack in the Democratic primary. Frank Kresini, an Allentown policeman whom Jack had demoted, was also mentioned. Democratic County Chairman Edward Galgon cryptically noted in the party newsletter that Jack and the few other party incumbents had "won the plaudits of the people and should be returned to office." Jack had earned loyalty from the party organization starting with his victory in the 1959 primary, and he used that support to take virtual control of the party when Galgon suddenly resigned in the spring of 1963. Jack's choice for a replacement, Joseph Spirk of Fountain Hill, was designated as the new chairman by the party executive committee at Jack's insistence. Then, when more opposition surfaced at the county committee meeting, Jack threatened to appear and nominate Spirk himself. That threat unnerved the opposition, and Spirk was unanimously elected to succeed Galgon in June 1963.

Jack's dominance of the local party structure was now complete. Hock had been fobbed off with a state job at the Public Utilities Commission, and Kresini chose to run for City Council, where he won the Democratic nomination for one of two seats. Jack was triumphantly re-nominated for mayor without opposition in the May primary. But Kresini's win, together with the nomination of J. Raymond Cramsey for the other seat by the Democrats, presented Jack with a real political dilemma. His party had nominated a mortal enemy in Kresini and a go-it-alone in Cramsey. Neither would be a friend and ally on council if elected. In fact, Kresini's primary campaign promise was to put Jack's public-housing projects before the city voters as a referendum before they were allowed to go forward. A referendum on public housing would have fatally delayed Jack's entire redevelopment plan and ripped apart the consensus he had built at the same time.

The solution Jack chose was to ignore his council running mates and trust that the more powerful Republican organization would reelect his ally, Snyder, and Lloyd Grammes, whom he disliked, but felt he could "handle" on major issues. As with almost everything in 1963, the strategy worked. He and the two Republicans were easily reelected.

Jack's overall strategy for the Democrats, which he termed "pick off the outriders" (meaning, take on only the weaker Republican office holders), also worked. Democrat Donald E. Wieand was elected Common Pleas Judge, and for the first time in 24 years, the Democrats took control of the County Commissioners, with Jack's ally, George Stahl, winning along with party stalwart LeRoy "Pop" Werley. Three Democrats also were elected to the powerful Allentown School Board.

The year 1963, however, was far more than just a good year politically for Jack. It was the most successful year of his life and arguably the city's as well.

In a New Year's Day interview with the *Evening Chronicle*, Jack had laid out his plans for Allentown. He noted that 1963 would be "something special," predicting massive accomplishments on three fronts. Now that center city had been cleared of buildings, a new City Hall would rise on Hamilton Street. A hundred units of townhouses and apartments would go up in the same area. Jack and his allies, (Phil Berman, Cy Gutman and developer Norman Denny,) saw apartments and particularly the high rise as the answer to the city's inability to otherwise expand its population. Denny even predicted great high rises at Center Square. Coupled with these apartment towers in center city would be others at 15th and Hamilton and near Trexler Park.

Apartments had become the mayor's answer to the lack of undeveloped city land for housing. There was, however, a fatal flaw in this hope. Apartments didn't serve the needs of the families who lived in the many blocks of row houses that formed the backbone of Allentown. The blue-collar workers and their children who lived in those homes wanted larger houses with two-car garages and yards with grass, not apartments with no yards. Jack never grasped Americans' love of green grass. He hated lawns and happily paved the few square feet of back yard of his 17th Street home so he could rid himself of his lawn mower. Most Americans in the 1960s were quite different. They had moved to the city for its better housing and jobs. Now they wanted those things, plus a big yard and a two-car garage as well.

The snowstorm that hit the city a year later demonstrated the problems that Allentown's system of row homes with one-car garages in the rear alleys caused when families owned two cars. One of those cars needed to be parked on the street, and if that street was a snow-emergency route, the car became a problem for the street crews. The

71

result was a mess of clogged streets when a snowstorm hit in January 1964. Jack's refusal to ticket many of the parked cars indicated that he sensed that the city's "people" could not be forced, by police pressures, to quickly move their second cars. Jack opted to favor leniency over efficiency in moving traffic because he believed people needed "a fair chance to dig out," no matter what the city snow ordinances said.

The same problem had surfaced in Jack's first term when city ordinances were proposed against cars being repaired or washed on streets. Opposition to those ordinances came from local labor leaders who complained that the city's row houses and alleys left their members nowhere else to fix and work on their second cars—an argument some newly arrived Latino residents also used 30 years later.

West of Allentown, Michael Gatti was about to give the city's row-home dwellers space, yards and garages in his new Ancient Oak development in Lower Macungie near Route 222; with the cars Mack workers could now afford, the distance to the South Side plant was no longer a problem. Gatti's price of $12,000 to $16,000 was also attainable with the new FHA and V.A. mortgages. Without space to meet the Ancient Oak concept, Allentown was doomed to lose more and more of its vital working-class residents. With no zoning or planning codes in the suburbs, it was cheap and easy to buy a farm and quickly build single-family homes with two-car garages on its already cleared fields.

The West End's grand homes continued to be the most desirable in the county into the late 1980s, and the new upscale apartments proposed for 15th and Hamilton and Trexler Park complemented those grand homes nicely, but the great masses of "the people" who stocked the city's vitals were slowly leaking to Ancient Oak and the other housing developments that quickly followed it. There was no effective response to that leak, which became a flood in the 1970s.

Worse, the grand apartments Jack hoped for downtown never really materialized, and the single-family row homes gradually became crowded apartments as the neighborhoods died. Allentown's population was misleadingly maintained, but not its "people" as Jack knew them.

Jack also looked for more industrial growth in 1963 now that Queen City Industrial Park was announcing one new industry after another. But the city had reached a point where it could count its available industrial land at barely 100 acres. As with housing, there was no real answer. Jack did note, hopefully, that the city had water and sewer facilities, which industry needed and the suburbs lacked. Later in 1963, he was to try to use this last card to force additional annexation from South Whitehall Township, and he also secretly negotiated with Bethlehem Mayor Gordon Payrow about dividing up Lehigh County's Hanover Township between the two cities. When those efforts failed, there was simply nowhere left to put new industry in Allentown.

Meanwhile, to preserve Hamilton Street shopping, Jack looked to a spur route directly from Route 22 to Hamilton Street to keep customers coming straight into town without the opportunity to stop in the growing suburbs. The spur route never happened, but the city kept trying throughout the year with a master traffic plan that included more one-way streets, parking meters and Park & Shop lots. Even street lighting was drastically changed from the city's famous lampposts. Larger new lights were to be erected to provide more light and safety on the street. The ultimate result was that neighborhoods around the center city died, as people fled from homes now on high-speed streets with vapor lights and parking meters.

More to the moment, 1963 was a golden year. In March, the State Supreme Court declared Jack's new job-privilege tax legal, which added $250,000 of surplus to the city budget. Earlier in the year, the new tax had been warmly praised at the Pennsylvania Municipal Finance Officers Association. Today, it is hard to imagine that any tax or its inventor would be considered praiseworthy, but Jack's tax gave the city the opportunity to tax those who worked in Allentown, but lived in the suburbs. That note sounded sweet to city dwellers.

More good news came from Mack Trucks, which finally announced in February that it would permanently stay and grow in Allentown. Jack welcomed the announcement with one of his own: A new "Mack" public pool would be built in the "long neglected" South Side. "None better" would be found in the eastern part of the state. Many city children spent most of their summer at these pools, which were viewed quite rightly as vital to each neighborhood. The South Side was now to have one of its own.

Meanwhile, concrete was poured for City Hall, and the Allentown Planning Commission finally approved plans for the townhouses development on South Fourth Street known as Hamilton Square. Jack greeted the approval with a dramatic commitment of his own. He and Agnes would be Hamilton Square's first tenants.

Even the brief delay in approval by the city planning commission caused Jack to threaten one of his now-signature personal appearances before the commission if it further delayed approval. Once again, the tactic worked. Jack was more and more displaying both impatience with any delay of his projects and willingness to take political risks to move them ahead.

Again, the mayor's personal commitment and constant face-to-face pressure had given him what he wanted quickly. Next, he used the same technique with the Allentown City Zoning Hearing Board, dining with its members before meetings to let them know exactly what the city wanted that night, and then sitting in the front row of the audience to make sure the board followed through. It invariably did.

If 1962 was the year of the Bicentennial, 1963 was the year of the All-America City. Ironically, Jack had originally disliked the former and only tacitly encouraged the latter. The All-America City award was a product of the Allentown-Lehigh County Chamber of Commerce efforts. The submittal to the National Municipal League and *Look* magazine featured Jack's redevelopment project, and the fact that the chamber felt confident enough to attempt it said volumes about attitudes in Allentown by 1963.

The award was made public March 28, and was followed by more celebrations, flag raisings and parades. Jack promised to use the honor as a "national advertising vehicle" for his industrial development program. Festivities culminated in a banquet on April 22 for 1,000 people with the state's new governor, Republican William Scranton, as the featured speaker at Muhlenberg's new Seegers Union.

Republican State Senator John T. Van Sant's resolution praising his home city in Harrisburg brought Northampton County State Senator Fred B. Rooney, a Democrat, forward with some good-natured political controversy. Rooney added Jack's name to the resolution of congratulations to which Van Sant quickly countered that Jack had been elected with the help of a whole lot of Republicans.

Rooney, who went on to Congress, had been at the hospital as soon as Jack's first heart attack was made public and was terribly shaken by the whole event. Jack was never, however, quite sure how to take the young Irishman from Northampton County and never got the time to find out what a strong and useful ally Rooney could be.

Another by-product of the award was the virtual endorsement for another term by the *Call-Chronicle's* legendary managing editor, William D. Reimert. As Jack accepted the presentation of the award, Reimert, the dinner's toastmaster, quipped that it "would benice if Mayor Gross were mayor of the city so he could hang this award in the new City Hall when it opens." Since City Hall was scheduled for completion in 1964, this remark, which pointedly appeared in the *Chronicle* the next day, made the newspaper's choice obvious even in a day when the ownership didn't formally endorse local candidates.

Jack's election victory on November 5 was huge. He carried every precinct, polling 21,467 votes to defeat the Republican candidate, former Mayor Brighton Diefenderfer, by almost two-to-one. He was the first mayor since his father, in 1927, to be reelected to consecutive terms.

Diefenderfer had honorably avoided public housing and instead pointed to "no comfort station" on Center Square as the key issue of his campaign. This seemingly silly small-town controversy in the All-America City hid two less obvious issues. The public comfort station on the square was councilman Ritter's responsibility, and on May 1, the Board of Health had recommended the men's facility be closed as a health hazard. As a result, Jack and his allies on council had an opportunity to taunt their nemesis for mismanagement.

The closing also gave Jack a political opportunity. The comfort station was run by Jack's Democratic opponent on the Democratic County Committee, Edward Gianetta. If it closed, Gianetta would lose his job. Gianetta was a former friend and supporter in the 1959 primary, but all that had changed by 1963, and the two men were now bitter rivals.

Gianetta actively opposed Jack's choice of County Chairman Spirk and generally fought Jack on Democratic Party matters. With the closing of the comfort station, Jack showed he could be punitive (and perhaps petty) by voting to reject Gianetta's request for a city pension. Although he claimed he was simply following legal advice from Republican City Solicitor Bernard Naef, he clearly enjoyed putting Gianetta in the difficult position of having to sue for his own pension.

A closing that Jack hoped to avoid, on the other hand, was the Allentown Public Library. Since December of the previous year, the trustees of the Allentown Free Library Association had been engaged in a game of chicken with the school board and city council with threats to close for shortage of funds. Jack and his ally, Dick Snyder, rejected the idea of a city takeover of the library. A tax increase would be necessary to fund its operations. At the same time, Jack privately pushed the school district to take over the association. He correctly gauged that board members would never risk the public condemnation if the library closed, he was right. After many shifts in position, the school board acted to take over the library. Jack's thanks to the board took a concrete form when he pasted together an odd coalition with Snyder and Grammes against Ritter and Fenstermacher to close 14th Street at Sumner Avenue, and thereby to save the district a million dollars in construction costs for its proposed new junior high school. Construction of the new school, "Trexler," only added to the euphoria of constant progress.

The failure of the library as a private charity, coupled with earlier pleas that the city might be required to take over the hoary institution of the Lehigh County Agricultural Society, which ran the Allentown Fair, was a signal that the city's private institutions were slowly failing under the weight of the cost required to keep going privately. Sensing that the city could never afford to take on the costs of maintaining operations for libraries and fairs, Jack also resisted this entreaty for a takeover. Yet, he knew how important they were and found other ways to help them. Somehow the fair and library survived.

In late November came the terrible news of John F. Kennedy's assassination. Jack, like most Americans, could only express his feelings of shock "beyond any semblance of cohesive comment." America and Allentown were never quite the same again.

III

On New Year's Day (1964), the *Evening Chronicle* published its annual interview with Jack on things to come in the city during the year. There was a good deal to be completed and much of the future to be planned in the next year, according to the triumphant mayor. Apartments and townhouses around Trout Hall, a motor inn (the future "Hamilton Plaza" at 4th and Hamilton Streets) and "expansions of old factories" and "newcomers" were all possible, according to Jack. He also noted, with no further detail, that 200 proposed low-income public-housing units would be built. That project was expected to be underway before the end of the year. No location was given.

Meanwhile, later that same month, Jack and Agnes moved into their new home at 45 S. 4th Street in the heart of the redevelopment area. Personal commitment was a vital part of Jack's style of government.

Jack's impatience continued as well. When council delayed a traffic light for access to the new Sarco plant along Lehigh Street in the Queen City Industrial Park, Jack told the press it was "embarrassing." Jack's ally, Republican council member Dick Snyder, agreed, but Bill Ritter was able to gain another delay. Jack seemed to sense that any delay used up time, which he no longer had. Awards, like a distinguished service plaque from the Chamber of Commerce, did little to placate his growing anger at what seemed inordinate slowness by the public bodies and council in acting on his plans for remaking the city. Jack had already decided he was in his final term as mayor, and was determined to complete every item on his personal agenda in the time left him. Ironically, he now almost consciously began to shorten his own life. His smoking was back to three packs a day. His drinking, including over lunch, was also up. News photos showed the once young-appearing mayor as heavy jowled with darkened eyes. Still, he rushed from store opening to meeting to dinner, showing himself wherever he was asked, but strangely, still feeling uncomfortable in the role he chose for himself. Paradoxically, the more uncomfortable and more tense he became, the more he played the hand he had dealt himself.

Then, in March, two great political storms broke on him. He had determined to run for governor in 1966. He had no known plan for how this impossible goal could be accomplished from politically insignificant Allentown. But on March 9, in what the *Chronicle* described as "an unscheduled address" to a labor rally on the steps of the capitol in Harrisburg, he read a speech attacking the Scranton administration's unemployment compensation bill as "misleading and often fraudulent." Jack said he had been asked by his friend, Harry Boyer, head of the state AFL-CIO, "to say something about the

... bill." From a prepared text, Jack then proceeded to blast Governor Scranton for "attacks on labor."

Jack's first foray into state politics hit Allentown hard the next day. Allentown mayors were expected to represent the entire town, not any one political party. Mal and then Jack had used the tremendous goodwill and prestige generated by this role to advance their projects. Both had, almost as an aside, also supported the Democratic Party, but neither had ever attempted to project themselves outside the city for political purposes. Using the mayor's prestige for a partisan issue outside the city was not part of the office's mystique. Jack now attempted to do just that, and on behalf of big labor to boot. He immediately learned the limits of his bipartisan support.

The following day the *Chronicle* expressed surprise and almost hurt in calling his attack an "error," especially from this "moderate" politician. The next day the *Call* hit much harder, calling Jack hysterical in his attacks on the governor.

These editorials were an ominous sign from two newspapers that, although Republican, they had not criticized Jack during his entire first term. More important, both papers had devoted daily space to educating the city's populace on Jack's new programs, laying the groundwork for their approval.

Both papers followed up with an embarrassing story on how the mayor had, as a member of the industrial development board, signed a letter supporting virtually the same legislation in 1963. Confronted on the contradiction, Jack told the *Chronicle* that he had changed his position. He somewhat illogically blamed the use of his old Department of Commerce by Scranton to promote the legislation, with attacks on labor as the reason for his change of heart. He claimed that by doing so, the Scranton administration had made the department "political."

Jack's speech on the capitol steps may have been no more than another of his increasingly frequent bursts of anger resulting in a confrontation with opponents (in this case, the governor himself). There is, however, another possible explanation. Jack's appearance was not on the labor rally's agenda, and by keeping his speech quiet, Jack may have hoped to win union support in his future race for governor while avoiding publicity at home. When his plan failed in that respect, he at least won local labor support from Anthony "Rocky" Stellar in the Allentown United

Auto Workers newsletter and from the needle trades, who stuck their thumb in the *Call's* eye by buying an advertisement on March 13 in the paper itself, thanking Jack for his support. But Jack needed total community support to push through his redevelopment program, and he couldn't have that support and play a role on the state political stage at the same time. He would need to choose between mayor and governor.

Whatever Jack's intent with his attack on Republican Scranton, he next rebuffed his own party leaders by supporting Genevieve Blatt for the U.S. Senate in the spring primary. In doing so, he set himself against his friends, former Governor Lawrence and Philadelphia boss Frank Smith. Smith had already offered his support for lieutenant governor to Jack in 1966, and Lawrence was always ready to help him. The party leaders endorsed Pennsylvania Supreme Court Justice Michael A. Musmanno for the Senate. Nevertheless, Jack, along with his close ally, Phil Berman, was named a vice-chairman of Blatt's upstart campaign committee.

Jack's endorsement of Blatt was rather strangely based, according to him, on Blatt's being an "old friend." Jack's commitment to Blatt, who won overwhelmingly in Lehigh County in the primary, made little sense for someone who hoped to run for governor in 1966, but he may have had no choice given Blatt's local popularity.

The 1964 primary split the Democratic party as Philadelphia and Pittsburgh bosses, trying to shore up their slipping Italian vote bloc, fought the rural and suburban wing led by U.S. Senator Clark and Blatt, who was one of the Democrats' most popular state vote-getters. It was a watershed election, and a loss from which the party's old guard never recovered.

The primary also confused and split the local party. Jack's ally, Chairman Spirk, loyally backed Musmanno. Louis D'Arconte, long-time opponent of both men, then announced he was running against Spirk as chairman, apparently based on Spirk's support of Musmanno. As a result, Jack was again forced to do an about face after the primary and personally nominate Spirk for reelection.

Jack's personal intervention papered over the crack he helped create, and Spirk was reelected. Two years later, Jack's powerful presence was gone forever, and real-estate man Glenn Moyer, with D'Arconte's support, took control of the local party for the rest of the century.

Meanwhile, however, a much more significant battle confronted the mayor. On March 9, 1964, the same day on which Jack made his attack on Scranton's unemployment-compensation bill, the housing authority announced the site for the 200-unit public-housing project made necessary by Jack's center city redevelopment. It chose a location in the South Side's 16th Ward on Carlisle Street. The location appeared ideal because only three homes were located on the entire tract. Furious opposition from the entire South Side developed immediately. Until the public-housing controversy of 1964, political disputes in Allentown had been played out in private, or like the comfort-station battle, fought over hidden issues that were rarely identified by the press or participants. The struggle over public housing was dramatically different. It was open, ugly and raw.

On the same day it blasted Jack for his attack on Governor Scranton's unemployment bill, the *Call* supported the public housing site. By March 12, the *Chronicle* was reporting major opposition in the 16th Ward to the idea. Residents called the idea a "sneak attack" like "Pearl Harbor" and "a real stab in the back." The initial focus of the opposition was the suddenness of the announcement and the lack of public input. For the time being Jack was not directly blamed. Instead, 16th Warders attacked council as a group and the housing authority. Jack initially deflected blame onto the authority, claiming he, too, was surprised when the authority came before council to announce its decision. But, shifting the blame to the decision-making process could not long delay questions about the location itself.

On March 17, a large delegation from the 16th Ward came before council represented by attorney James Kellar, who ended his presentation with, "let's put it across from your house." Location was now squarely the issue. Jack's response was that, although council had approved the site, it could be changed later. The fundamental problem facing Jack was now plain. In order to obtain money from the rapidly constricting pool of federal funds for his redevelopment projects, the city had to have public housing. As a result, Jack couldn't afford any delay in submittal of the Cumberland Gardens location to Washington.

For the first time in his political career, Jack faced real opposition from the "people" of the city. Apparently hoping to play for time, he was, in effect, proposing to mislead the federal government that the public housing site had been finally approved to obtain federal funding for redevelopment, but possibly changing the site later if another could be found, or misleading the South Side that change was still possible. It was a dangerous political game, but necessary to create cover for council and avoid its withdrawing support at a critical point in the program. With time, Jack hoped to educate the public and develop support for the concept of public-housing projects. Some help came immediately from Reverend George Yoder who boldly accused the opposition of "prejudice not in keeping with the All American City."

The 16th Warders, however, found a leader who was prepared to push the issue to the limit. LeRoy Bogert had recently lost a bid for the Republican mayoral nomination. He was to seek public office again and again in future years, always losing. He had a fire about him and a vision of Allentown, often a dark vision, which was to make him a figure to be reckoned with during the next decade. Partially bald with stray white locks of hair, he had an almost professorial look. Bogert had a gift for making dramatic statements that caught the mood of an angry public. He took up the South Side cause and stayed with it, demanding the one thing Jack could not give, an immediate rescindment of council's approval of the site. Bogert clashed heatedly at council meetings with Jack, who cut him off after Bogert called project tenants "degraded." Not surprisingly, Bogert quickly won Ritter's support, but the rest of council held firm to Jack's insistence on the need for further study.

Meanwhile, the project and redevelopment went forward, and with the city already land-poor, no other realistic site was possible no matter how much study took place. Using the time council's support gave him, Jack began a public-education campaign, which cleverly met the publicly advanced objections of the 16th Warders. This tactic of taking the opposition at its word that it was not fighting the project based on race or poverty, but rather on whether the site had suitable roads, schools and public services, forced the South Siders into a corner. Jack had control of the facts of those issues, and he mobilized masses of information to demonstrate that the project presented no problems. Allentown School District responded to inquiries that the schools in the area were "adequate" and would be expanded if necessary. Similar support for Jack's position was to come shortly.

On March 22, the Human Relations Commission issued a fact-laden statement rebutting the 16th Warders' claims. The statement had a double benefit. First, the public saw a detailed rebuttal of the arguments that housing already existed, that tax money would be wasted on the project, and property values would be depressed by public housing. Second, the signers included future political leaders like Reverend Grant Harrity and Jack McHugh, clergy like Rabbi Stephen A. Schafer of Congregation Kenneth Israel and Father Francis Donnelly of St. Catharine's, the city's largest Catholic church. Labor leaders like Isaac Gordon of the ILGWU also signed. Jack's earlier strategy of energizing the city authorities and commissions by stocking them with powerful leaders was obviously paying an additional dividend. Community leaders were virtually forced, by their public positions, to rally to Jack's side on public housing. Allentown was still a community, and a community that followed its leaders.

At the same time, Jack benefitted from continued council support. Ritter was not likely to be able to create a majority on any issue. He lacked a single friend on council. Bogert was a Republican maverick who had repeatedly broken tight party discipline by running in primaries and was disliked by his own party regulars. The key to the situation was a majority of votes on council, regardless of the South Side's anger. If Jack could hold two council votes in addition to his own, the public outcry was meaningless.

One of those votes quickly came from Lloyd Grammes, who announced that he would not be forced into a "snap judgment" to rescind council approval. Grammes picked up on Jack's earlier theme that people whose homes had been razed by the redevelopment project needed a place to live. Grammes also emphasized that the Cumberland Gardens site itself was vacant. Badly crippled from polio, sharp-tongued, cigar-chomping, career Allentown politician Grammes was the master of the closed-door political infighting in City Hall. His control of the large number of patronage jobs in the city's street department was absolute, and he had never been close to Jack. With his vote assured, Jack had only to hold onto his longstanding ally, Snyder, to make certain that council stayed with its earlier decision.

As a further part of his strategy to hold council together, but keep it from revoking its approval of the site, Jack began meeting with the Allentown Housing Authority to explore the possibility of other locations. Although he refused to identify the other sites "for obvious reasons," a wire mill property at the base of the Lehigh Street hill near the redevelopment area was the primary alternate location. Many 16th Warders had been making the argument that the new upscale housing occupants should have the displaced poor near them. This argument needed to be rebutted. Further, the explanation had to be for reasons like "terrain," not undesirability of the public housing tenants near the new apartments, to avoid the claims of elitism.

Only three days after the A.H.A. meeting, Jack joined the Republican majority in voting to reappoint an all-Republican solicitor's office. Ritter bitterly dissented, and called the GOP lawyers "negligent" over the Gianetta case, making Jack's job easier in holding together a majority for the public-housing project. Later, he was to link with all three Republicans on council to strip Ritter of a number of his bureaus and employees. Clearly, Bill Ritter's vote lost others on council on any issue, even public housing.

More support for the project came when the board of directors for the Senior Citizen Center urged council to move ahead. Again community support was slowly building, thereby fencing in the 16th Ward opposition. That opposition was, however, stimulated again on April 6th by federal approval of the project. Jack kept up his strategy of delay at home while matters moved quickly ahead in Washington. He continued to assure the 16th Ward residents who appeared before council only the day before that council was still waiting for the A.H.A. to look at the wire mill site. At the May 21st council meeting, Jack, although continuing to maintain that the actual location was up to the A.H.A., categorically refused to back down on the immediate need for a public housing project.

By June it was clear that the authority would not approve a change in the site to the Wire Mill area because of flooding problems. Jack's strategy of claiming the site location was up to the authority, while he pushed it through the federal bureaucracy in Washington had worked. Cumberland Gardens was to become a reality.

With success on the first redevelopment project came the announcements by Rod Terry, the authority's new director, that another much larger, 100-acre project would begin shortly near the first project. Significantly, the public housing component of that phase was ultimately located on the Lehigh Street hill—within the redevelopment area, not in another part of the city. The politicians had learned their lesson from the Cumberland Gardens' fight.

The balance of the summer of 1964 permitted Jack to direct his attention to moving to the new City Hall, which opened for business in August. He proudly posed for a newspaper photo in his top floor office from which he noted he could see almost all of his Allentown.

Two last honors, which had escaped Mal, remained for Jack in the last month of his life. On August 12th, he was elected president of Pennsylvania's League of Cities. In Jack's acceptance speech, perhaps looking to the 1966 governor's election, he described himself as being "appalled" at the way the State Legislature and Governor ignored the "nearly one-half of the population" living in the cities.

Perhaps more important to Jack personally was his selection as a delegate to the Democratic National Convention in Atlantic City. Mal's only election loss in his long political career had been for delegate to the 1924 convention; Jack often mentioned that defeat and engineered his selection for a fractional delegate vote by the Democratic State Committee. But Jack's last hope that he would at least be able to vote "on something" at a national convention was never fulfilled. Lyndon Johnson was nominated by acclamation. Jack returned to Allentown exhausted, and for the first time, admitted to worrying about his weak heart. A visit to his heart specialist quickly reassured him, and he headed off to yet another evening meeting.

On September 3, 1964, Jack suffered his fatal heart attack. He had moved to his new City Hall office only 30 days before.

With Jack's death, Bill Ritter became acting mayor by virtue of the old City Charter, which Mal had written. The irony was lost on city residents overwhelmed by genuine and deep grief. Jack, who promised them greatness again and delivered much of it in five tremendously busy years, was gone.

Flag Burning
July, 1989

This was my first venture into national controversial themes. At the time, it appeared the world was going to end if the Constitution was not amended to prevent flag burning by overruling a recent Supreme Court of the United States decision. The amendment proposed by President George H. Bush had a good deal of popular support at the time of this publication on July 9, 1989. I was, therefore, quite nervous about the reaction. Immediately after it appeared, however, I was approached by one of the court personnel who congratulated me vigorously on taking my stand. Later, I heard, quietly as usual, from a number of other people who felt that I was on the right track. President Bush's amendment never got off the ground, and the country has survived.

Flag burning is bad. A constitutional amendment to ban flag burning is worse than bad. It is foolish. Gregory Lee Johnson burned an American flag in front of Dallas City Hall during the 1984 Republican Convention. As he did so, he, and a group of protesters, chanted, "America, the red, white and blue, we spit on you." No disturbance, riot, or breach of the peace occurred as Johnson's ugly little drama was unfolding. However, several bystanders later testified they were offended by the flag burning.

Because of the bystanders' hurt feelings, not because of Johnson's actions themselves, Texas prosecuted him for desecration of a "venerated object." Johnson was convicted, sentenced to a year in prison, and fined $2,000. Recently, the U.S. Supreme Court upheld a Texas appeals court decision reversing Johnson's conviction and ruled, by a 5-4 vote, that the Texas law in question violated the First Amendment.

Congress, which has been unable to deal with its own ethical mess, the savings and loan bailout, or the Exxon oil spill, finally found something it could deal with. Constitutional amendments by the score were immediately introduced. And Representative Newt Gingrich (R-Georgia) asserted that a vote against the amendments "would be hard to explain" to the voters back home. Patriotism was in the air.

President Bush, who had been pleading for Congressional restraint as hundreds of Chinese students were killed by their own army, initially reacted with caution. He said he opposed the flag decision, but as president would uphold it. Political considerations quickly changed his mind. The president now offered his own constitutional amendment. It read "The Congress and the states shall have the power to prohibit the physical desecration of the flag of the United States."

Fortunately, amendment of our Constitution is not an easy thing. First, two-thirds of both the House and Senate must give their approval. After that approval, 38 state legislatures must separately approve the amendment as well. Obviously, a great deal of political energy and time is consumed by such a cumbersome process. Political energy and time are not inexhaustible resources. The question, then, is whether they should be spent on this or some other issues.

In order to answer that question, it is important to understand the Supreme Court's decision that sparked the controversy. When Gregory Lee Johnson burned a flag and chanted his rhyme, he was using conduct as speech to attack the government. The First Amendment protects free speech against government interference. In short, whether we like what they say or not, we can't put people in jail for saying the government is rotten.

The problem under the First Amendment is when do actions as well as words make the same point. When those actions are violent or likely to provoke violence the answer is easy – the First Amendment does not apply, and the government has the authority to prosecute those responsible. However, many other actions intended as speech present a much more difficult question. An anti-abortion march, for example, is a form of speech on a national issue even if the marchers keep absolutely silent during their walk. The marchers are making a statement by their action; therefore, the government cannot ban such a march because of the First Amendment.

It was this hard question – of when conduct becomes speech – that confronted the Supreme Court in the flag-burning case. In addition, the situation was complicated because Texas had prosecuted Johnson for the effect his flag burning had on several spectators, not because he burned a flag. Apparently, had Johnson burned his flag at home among friends who thought it was a wonderful idea, no crime would have occurred under Texas law.

One simple solution was possible in Johnson's case. The court could have adopted the theory of the late liberal Justice Hugo Black and drawn a bright line between speech and action. Justice Black believed the First Amendment protected all spoken or written words no matter how obscene or offensive – but nothing else. The act of burning a flag would be, therefore, not part of the First Amendment, and Johnson could be sent to jail for it. The problem with such an approach is that the silent anti-abortion marchers could also be sent to jail.

As a result, the court has, in the past, permitted people to say and do insulting things, about and to the flag. Attaching a peace sign to the flag and wearing a flag on the seat of your pants, for instance, have been held to be protected by the First Amendment.

In any event, given the peculiar facts of the case and its past precedent, five of the court's members felt they had little choice except to declare Johnson's conduct as symbolic speech under the first Amendment. The majority's discomfort with the result is evidenced by Justice Anthony Kennedy's sad concurring opinion calling the decision "painful." Four justices attempted to avoid the problem caused by 'conduct-as-speech' by arguing the flag was so special a symbol of our country that acts involving it were not covered by the First Amendment even where they were intended and understood as a criticism of the government.

All nine justices seem to have agreed, as Professor Lawrence Tribe has pointed out, that the government still can constitutionally prohibit all flag burning, public or private. Thus, any state can pass a law saying that one cannot burn a flag anywhere without a new constitutional amendment. States also can continue to bar vandalism and breach of the peace regarding the flag. Therefore, we don't need the Bush Amendment unless, for the first time ever, we also wish to limit our right to free speech under the First Amendment.

The Constitution has never been amended to limit the Bill of Rights. The Bush Amendment would do so for the first time in our history. Do we really want or need to do that? Are we really concerned with protecting the flag, or our ears, from unpleasant, but free speech?

Regardless of which side was right on what is a rather narrow matter in the Johnson case, we don't need to spend our next year listening to state and national politicians praise the flag. They have more important work to do regarding their own ethics and a whole raft of domestic and foreign issues.

In addition, an important Supreme Court decision on abortion recently seemed to reopen that critical issue in every one of our state legislatures. The abortion issue and the others like it will take all the time and political energy we have without a flag-burning amendment.

Muhlenberg College and Neighborhood Zoning
December, 1998

This piece apparently landed like a bomb on the Muhlenberg campus. It was greeted by a sarcastic reply article from two members of the administration, the denunciation of me at a college event by the president, a letter to the Editor from the Chairman of Board of Trustees, and a more or less total break with the college. That was all painful for a bit, but I must admit I enjoyed the controversy and am now back in the Muhlenberg fold.

Muhlenberg College's recent decision to appeal the Lehigh County court's decision against it under the City's new restrictive zoning ordinance around the school is foolish and counterproductive. It is foolish because the college stands little or no chance of reversing Judge Lawrence Brenner's decision against it, and it is counterproductive because it will place the College in a position of standing alone with a city and neighborhood united against it. If Muhlenberg goes forward with the appeal in what appears to be its present policy of escalating its dispute with its own neighborhood, it will become a college merely located in Allentown, not part of Allentown. I make that statement as a member of a family that has sent four generations, beginning in 1894, through the college's red doors.

Legal costs, by themselves, in this case will be enormous for the college; however, the political and community costs in terms of Muhlenberg's relationship with Allentown will be far worse if it continues on its current course. To change that course, Muhlenberg needs to recognize, and then make others recognize, some very fundamental facts.

There are three parties to this case - the college, the city, and the neighbors. However, it is not the number of parties that makes this case unique and vital for Muhlenberg, it is the impossibility of any litigant "winning" a neighborhood zoning dispute. Unlike every other case in which one side pays money and the other side goes away, neighbors always remain in place after a lawsuit. They are there every day and every night either triumphant in their legal victory or embittered by what they will regard as a temporary setback, but they are always there.

But the worst thing for all three parties is that the neighbors and the city also stand to "lose big time" in this litigation. Muhlenberg is also not going anywhere. It will be in its current location no matter what happens in its appeal. All sides, including the city, will remain in place no matter what happens in any appeals court.

It is this simple truth that all three parties need to recognize so that they can look past their legal disputes to the fundamental problem of a rapidly expanding college (Muhlenberg has over 100 more freshman this year than it expected) in a sadly declining, but proud old neighborhood. Neighbors counting student cars, college tax appeals to save a few dollars of real estate taxes, and constant police calls to the city will only make the situation worse. Someone has to have the strength and courage to reach out for real peace in the West End.

Arthur Taylor, Muhlenberg's President, is the only member of this cast of characters who is in a position to do so. He controls his college's actions in a way the politicians and neighbors don't. They can only react to what he does.

President Taylor should immediately make a unilateral gesture to everyone and drop, without condition, the college appeal. He should also announce exactly what the long range college plans are for its student population, explain where the college will house those students, and pledge his personal word that the college will stick to those plans. If city help or neighborhood understanding is needed for the college to grow and thrive, within those plans, the President needs to say publicly exactly what that need is now. Once that's done, the college will have seized the moral high ground, and that is the only place to be in this kind of a political dispute.

More important, long range, the college needs to become the primary positive force solving the real problem in the decline in West End real estate values - the city's school system. If the neighbors and politicians come to believe that Muhlenberg, like Trinity College in Hartford, has directed all of its outside efforts, including its own endowment, into upgrading Allentown's public schools with specific meaningful ideas, the whole perception of what Muhlenberg is about in this town will change. That change in perception will make it possible for Muhlenberg to, once again, become part of its own neighborhood.

In 1920, when the great Spanish flu epidemic laid low the city's teachers, Muhlenberg students filled in for them to keep the schools open. Bureaucracy and unions wouldn't allow that kind of simple effective step today. But long term, there are many meaningful effective efforts the college could make to revitalize Allentown's much disparaged school system. That's where Muhlenberg should be directing its efforts, not on the zoning appeal.

Election "store card" of my father for his re-election campaign in 1963.
He deliberately copied his father's card promoting **"Mal" Gross for Mayor**.

The Electoral College
January, 2001

I did not play much of a role in the 2000 presidential election,
although my wife Janet and I supported Gore and followed the fiasco of
Bush winning as a minority president with dismay. I offered this piece
as a possible compromise. I was ignored here and elsewhere.

When my wife and I visited Germany two weeks before the debacle that was to become the recent presidential election, I was asked by German friends to predict the outcome. I guessed Bush would win, and then mentioned that the Electoral College could change the result. Our friends were amazed. Was the U.S. really a democracy? Had America not twice defeated the Germans to make the world safe for a form of government that it didn't believe in? Several beers and many sausages later, I was still unable to answer those questions. I still can't, and after what happened since, I now ask why not get rid of this hoary horror.

The Morning Call, in a post-election editorial, disagreed with me and Republican Senator Arlen Specter who also wants to abolish the college. *The Morning Call* argues that the college is the product of an historic compromise by the founding fathers to insure that the small states were not dominated by the rest. That was not the reason for the college. The Electoral College was set up to guarantee that the slave states controlled the executive. The Constitution gave them a 3/5 credit in population apportionment for their slaves. Those extra fractions meant that a slave owner was president for 40 of the first 48 years of the republic. The small states were protected in the original Constitution by giving them two senators, regardless of population, which they still have - not votes in the college. That's enough.

The Civil War settled the issue of slavery, and the 15th Amendment in 1870 made it official. African Americans were real people who could vote like all other men. That started a trend toward democratic values determining who governed America. Women in 1920, and eighteen year olds, who were fighting the Vietnam War in 1971, were constitutionally classified as "people" as well, and given the vote. Meanwhile, the courts in the 1960s required complete democracy in state governments with one man one vote.

Yet the most anti-democratic of all our institutions, the Electoral College, remained firmly in place probably because it had done no perceived harm since 1888 when it made Harrison president despite Cleveland winning the popular vote. As a result, the poison pill in the Constitution was overlooked. Campaigns for president continued to be waged in the few states the pollsters told the candidates were crucial in the college. Then came Election 2000.

Gore won the popular election by well over 500,000 votes, but chads and the Supreme Court did him in. Florida cast its electoral votes for "W" who is now president. Bush took office already badly weakened by scandal and impeachment, and now flawed by a result contrary to every democratic principle. Like Gore - it is time for the college to go.

Democracy is on the move worldwide -for good reason. It's getting to be impossible to run a major nation and economy unless everybody agrees who runs the government. Religion and ideology are no longer an excuse for excluding people from power. Yet democracy lags behind in the presidency — the only office that represents all of us.

The Morning Call's second reason for keeping the college was that the small states will never give it up which is also misplaced. Whites gave blacks the vote; men gave it to women; over 21 year olds to 18 year olds. Each group acted against its own short-term self-interest for the long-term common good. The problem is not with the small states. The problem is party politics. Like all-important constitutional matters, significant change occurs in America only when there is bipartisan agreement. The lack of such agreement is why we can't get rid of the college. First the Democrats and now the Republicans cling to the hope that they may benefit in some future election from it. If the parties agree to a change, the small state legislatures they control will quickly do the same.

That's where President Bush comes in. He can immediately call for the end of the Electoral College. In one gesture, he can make himself legitimate by saying he will fight his next election based on a popular vote. In one gesture, he can demand the type of meaningful bipartisanship which he says is crucial. If he does so, the Democrats will have no choice but to follow or lose their party's very name.

That would mean the 2004 election would really be held all over America, not in ten or twenty states the pollsters tell the candidates are necessary to swing the college. That would mean a vote in Texas would count the same as Maine. The campaign would truly be national in scope.

That would mean democracy would finally come to America.

Two Mayors and a Lawyer

Ignore Ghosts of Downtown
February, 1997

I tried to get the Lehigh Valley past its daydreams about the good old days of Hess's and "The Street" and alert them to a new reality for the city. Encouraged by some pats on the back at my favorite lunch place on Hamilton Street I wrote this piece, which actually got a letter to the Editor, a cartoon, and more comments.

When my wife and I visited Rome, I thought that it must be a strange experience living in the middle of a city with great ruins literally next door. Now I feel a bit like the modern Romans myself. From the window of my fourth floor office on South Seventh Street, I literally, or figuratively, see Hess Brothers Department Store, the Good Spirit Restaurant, the Colonial Theatre, the Lehigh Portland Cement Building, the Plaza Hotel, and the ruins of H. Leh & Company. I never saw Christians eaten by lions in any of those places, but I do remember many happy moments in them. Now, they are also all closed and a bit like the Coliseum to those who must live and work around them. As a result, I have come to see anecdotal conclusions about "downtown".

First, there is no longer a "downtown" in Allentown. There is only a street called Hamilton on which are located those empty buildings, which I mentioned above and many other empty buildings and a combination of some rather sad stores. Having events which draw the public to see what's here is now like drawing lightning to yourself. Major retail merchandising is dead and buried in "downtown." It lives on MacArthur Road and on Cedar Crest Boulevard where the necessary critical mass of malls, autos, and shoppers is concentrated.

Second, Allentown's "downtown" is lacking in significant charm or historic significance. Granted, there are some lovely buildings and a few places of historic interest. However, the type of quaint structures which makes downtown Bethlehem worth saving is simply not present in Allentown.

Downtown Allentown looks like what it was – a commercial district erected mostly in the twentieth century to serve shoppers and businesses. It is not particularly pretty, and the effort to "save" it in the 1970s with the metal canopies of Hamilton Mall has now made it even less so.

Third, I'm about consulted out. The numerous studies which have been visited on us in the last fifteen years are worse than worthless. Those studies and the consultants who wrote them raised completely unrealistic expectations and now only serve to create more cynicism.

I worked my way through despair about the downtown several years ago. I still believe it has potential, but only if we are realistic and attempt to appreciate what's actually here.

There is still a center city, if not a downtown. If we think about the center of Allentown and work from that point, we have a realistic chance of success with what is here and could be here. That means we have to ignore Hamilton Street and look at what exists in the blocks that form the middle of town.

We need to attempt to identify what is working here. Too much time has been spent on trying to start new things. Instead, we need to identify what is here and succeeding in being here. We may have a great many closed buildings from the past, but we also have a number of successful operations. PP&L still employs thousands of people. The nearby hotel provides quality guest accommodations. Symphony Hall sells out musical concerts. The Art Museum is outstanding, and the Public Library is tops. There are also a surprising number of good small shops.

Surprisingly, there has also been a fair amount of major construction. A federal courthouse has just been completed; a county office building is well underway; *The Morning Call* underwent a major expansion; Sacred Heart Hospital is about to begin construction on a new office building; and Central Catholic High School is completing a major renovation. Someone needs to cooperate with and expand on these successes. We also need to know why these things happened in the face of the general decline.

Next, we need to know what it will take to keep and expand those entities which are staying and succeeding. Too often we put out ideas such as tax-free zones without asking whether those ideas have any meaning for what is here. For instance, it means little to set up a tax free zone if the biggest successes in the area are churches, societies, and government entities, which already pay no taxes. We would do better to learn what business in center city needs, and then spend money and effort to meet those needs.

There's no longer any reason why we need to be crowded for space. Why not use all available economic strength to create campuses around the successes which we have, instead of allowing urban blight to exist next door. Tear down the blight for access parking and aesthetics. The cost would be far less than a "new" convention center, and it would enhance enterprises which are already working. That has already happened at the Liberty Bell Shrine where Mayor William Heydt got rid of the 1970s metal canopy, and the building next door was torn down.

If we couple such action with an effort to create affordable housing in center city so young people who work here can also live here, we have a chance to start building a new center city community. To make that happen we need to find out who they are, where they live now, and what it would take to get them to live within walking distance of center city.

Finally, there is still a lingering provincialism about Allentown. It is no longer a privilege to serve on our boards and commissions. The city can't expand its political boundaries, but it can expand its vision and recruit anyone who has an interest in what is going on here for its appointed bodies. That way, everyone in this Valley will have the opportunity to own a piece of the new center city community.

America's Only Philosophy - Pragmatism
February, 2002

I began to hit my stride as a writer with this piece on Enron and got invited to speak at DeSales University as a result.

"Truth is what works" is how one wit described America's only philosophy — pragmatism. To be pragmatic is to be hardheaded, practical, by taking the line of least resistance to get to an immediate objective. Fixed principles do not exist for the pragmatist. Pragmatism was first propounded as a philosophy by an obscure professor, Charles Peirce, over 100 years ago. Being pragmatic is both the highest compliment an American can receive and the nearest anyone has come to describing the American genius.

Enron was the ultimate example of pragmatism in business. It focused exclusively on forcing up its stock price. To do so it ignored law, ethics, and honesty. When any of those outdated fixed principles stood in the way of its objective, it simply got the government to change them, went around them, or bought its way through them. Enron was widely praised and its methods admired. Presidents played golf and exchanged personal greetings with Enron's CEO Kenneth Lay. Its highly paid Board of Directors included conservative Senator Phil Gramm's wife and a Texas Law School dean. It paid $50,000 for "advice" from liberal *New York Times* economist Paul Krugman. Politicians from both parties received huge donations from Enron. Two million dollars was contributed in the last four years to Senate and House members alone.

And it worked. Enron's stock price rose and rose. Wall Street's "analysts" recommended it. Enron's independent auditors were at the same time paid by it to be "consultants." Arthur Anderson certified to its financial soundness. If something worked, it must be true, the pragmatists said. Success was truth. Enron was true blue.

Then Enron suddenly failed. The other side of pragmatism's equation came into play. If success was truth then failure was falsity. Nothing can be learned from falsity, said America's pragmatic politicians. President Bush couldn't remember his friend Ken Lay's first name. The Democratic National Committee said it was giving back the last hundred thousand it got from Enron.

101

Abandon failure quickly, pragmatists told us. Move on to other successes.

But there are fixed principles in life, and failure is part of success. We can and should look at and try to remedy what went wrong with Enron in politics. We can and should face Enron's failure and learn from it and do something about it. The idea that the political money Enron used to buy access to the president's cabinet was unimportant because the cabinet didn't bail it out, is ridiculous. A political system that gives access to officials based only on money, will, at best, allow those with money to crowd out all others. At worst, government will do the bidding of the only voice it hears. The McCain-Feingold campaign finance reform bill will at least make a start toward banning soft money in political campaigns. Last week, 218 "idealists" in the House of Representatives forced it to the floor. However, House leaders, pragmatic as always, are already setting up a whole series of traps to defeat McCain-Feingold and keep the soft money flowing. They have boasted they will use all means from parliamentary tactics to poison pill amendments to get to their goal.

It's time for some old fashioned, fuzzy thinking, softheaded idealism. Campaign finance reform will never take all of the money out of politics. Like most ideals, it can never be completely achieved in this world. However, it is a start toward making politics based on something more than money. It is also a road back from Enron's pragmatism.

To paraphrase George Santayana, another American philosopher, those who don't know Enron are condemned to repeat it.

They Ask Me All the Time What I Think of "It"
June, 2002

This piece made me very nervous. The subject was at that time still very explosive. As a practicing Catholic, I wondered what the reaction would be in and out of the church locally. There was none from my clergy friends, but one member of the laity on the Sacred Heart Board said that I had gotten it just about right.

They ask me all the time what I think of "it." Friends, knowing I am a Roman Catholic, want to know my view on "it." Casual acquaintances upon learning my religion immediately bring "it" up. "It" is the sexual abuse scandal.

The scandal has three parts. First, about 20 years ago a significant, but still relatively small number of priests all over America sexually attacked the young Catholics entrusted to their care. It is hard to imagine a worse crime. Second, apparently, for the entire 20-year period some high Catholic officials covered up the crime and allowed the criminals to remain at large often committing more attacks. That is a very bad thing. Third, the American press, recognizing the public had finally read more than it wanted to about Congressman Gary Condit, pounced on every court filing, trial lawyer's statement, or Cardinal's gaff. Getting another story on "it" has become an end in itself.

Meanwhile, in a way I have never seen, the Church repeatedly apologized and asked the laity's support. The former is appropriate, and hopefully will soon be followed up with action nationally like that already taken in Allentown. The latter is impossible to do. This is not because there is no support — there is a great deal, particularly for pastors and priests who labor daily for the faith. Rather the laity's support is impossible because of what makes the Church unique, interesting, and important in the secular world — its structure. The Church structure is an absolute monarchy.

Except for my church, the absolute monarchy form of government doesn't exist today. Even the worst tyrannies are based on a façade of popular support. Hitler was democratically elected. The Taliban had a council of elders to vote on whether to give up Bin Laden. However, since at least 1870 when the Pope was declared infallible, all power in the Church rests unashamedly in one man. This makes for a very single-minded, focused, and principled institution in a modern world, which otherwise, has none of those things.

Nevertheless, in a crisis of this magnitude when popular support is vital, an absolute monarchy has no effective means to receive it. All power flows from the Pope. There is no way for power to run from the people to him or his appointed Cardinals. In other words, the Church has a governance problem. The obvious answer is to turn its structure into a democracy. That cannot happen.

The Church staked out its position on these issues at the time of the Protestant Reformation and has held steady to it for the last 400 years. It is still vital for its uniqueness in the modern world. Catholicism is "the Church" not "a church" because of the mystery of its Mass. That mystery can only exist with a separate priesthood, independent of lay control. If the Church becomes a democracy and the Pope a constitutional figurehead, the mystery protected by that separation will vanish and the uniqueness of the Mass with it.

Still, the Church is part of the popular world, and its structure cannot divorce it from its own people. It desperately needs them to survive as well.

The answer may lie in a recognition that there are worldly areas (administration and finance) in which lay input and even some control could serve a useful purpose without limiting the clergy's authority in spiritual areas. With the burden of control shared in the temporal areas, the Church's spiritual side could have more room to grow and thrive. In other words, render unto Caesar the things that are Caesar's.... An invitation from the hierarchy for some formal discussions with lay leaders about the Church's worldly issues would be a start in determining whether such a limited restructuring of the Church's governance is possible. There would be a risk that even discussion could open a Pandora's Box of recrimination. There would also be the obvious risk of failure. Both are significant. The Church has not thrived for 2000 years by jumping to quick fixes for its problems. However, the unfolding tragedy of its priests' sexual misdeeds is not going away, and a serious look at Church governance in secular areas might be more positive than the daily drumbeat of headlines and apologies.

What a Week at My Alma Mater Muhlenberg College!
July, 2002

Back came Muhlenberg into my life. This piece drew a comment from another local college president noting that I correctly analyzed the turnovers in the office of president at Berg.

What a week at my alma mater Muhlenberg College! After months (some say years) of controversy during the presidency of Arthur Taylor, it is suddenly over. Now comes the hard part for the board of trustees who, by the way, had no choice but to act on and then compromise with Taylor to end the bleeding. The difficulty is not finding a new president or deciding whether he or she needs a Ph.D. – it is dealing with the next decade at the college. Arthur leaves Muhlenberg in a healthy state, but each of his positives hides a major challenge.

First, enrollment has increased by over 400 students since Arthur took over. However, Muhlenberg is now wedded to that increase to balance its budget and justify the expansion of its campus. With a four year education costing parents over $130,000 at the college and job offers at even $30,000 to $40,000 per year hard to come by for this year's graduates, Muhlenberg, like other schools, could find it impossible to sustain the high enrollment and maintain its high standards at the same time.

Second, whether the three-fold increase in the endowment was due to Arthur's stewardship or the bull market of the 1990s, Wall Street is now in the tank. Natural growth, therefore, will not help the endowment, and donors no longer have inflated stocks to gift to the college. That means fundraising could be hard cheese in the next ten years.

Third, the rapid growth at the college has left bitter simmering disputes with Muhlenberg's immediate neighborhood and faculty. Some tension between town and gown as well as faculty and administration is always present in a college community. But, the open warfare of the immediate past must be ended. The same kind of common sense that ended the Taylor presidency will be needed, which is always easier said than done.

I don't agree, as an outsider, with *The Morning Call's* recent editorial criticism of the board's delay in firing Arthur Taylor. As a member of many nonprofit boards over the years, I know how difficult it is for volunteer board members to get a handle on a difficult situation especially with a powerful president. Regardless, the board did what it had to do, even if it, perhaps, should have done so earlier.

The Morning Call was, however, dead on point regarding the board's obligations to go forward. The board needs to take those obligations more seriously in the future.

Muhlenberg is presently a "hot school" for student recruitment. It doesn't need to beg for a new president. It can look for more than a "personality" or a "leader." Its board can decide where it wants to go on the challenges Arthur has left behind and some other issues as well. It can demand that those who wish to be its next president respond with ideas on how to get to the goals the board sets for the years ahead. In other words, before it starts its "search," the board should know where it wants the college to be in the next few years. Who takes over next is almost secondary. The destination is what matters. The past decade saw tame corporate and institutional boards and aggressive, dominating CEOs. We are now seeing a swing in the pendulum in the opposite direction. Boards are becoming more than fundraising vehicles bowing unquestioningly to their chiefs. They are taking responsibility with regard to the institutions they serve. Muhlenberg's board now has a chance to do the same.

One last thing. Muhlenberg seems to have trouble shedding its presidents. At least two presidents, since I graduated in the 1960s, left under less than pleasant circumstances before the present nearly complete fiasco. So why not also ask a new candidate for the job how long he believes it will take to achieve the goals the board sets, and use the candidate's time limit as a tentative end for his assignment as president as well? That way, we might actually be able to have a farewell party for the next president.

Lincoln's Gettysburg Address

November, 2002

As a Democrat interested in history, I spent most of my early years reading about Democratic presidents like Jackson, Cleveland, Wilson, FDR, Truman and Kennedy. I pretty much ignored Lincoln, TR and Eisenhower. About ten years ago, however, Lincoln caught my attention first as a lawyer and then as a legal philosopher.

November 19th is the anniversary of the most significant political event in America's nineteenth century history — Lincoln's Gettysburg Address. In 1863, with 272 words, Lincoln changed the dynamic of the American legal and political world for the next 110 years. Today, Lincoln's speech is viewed as kind of a funeral oration. It was even used last September 11th to commemorate that terrible tragedy. However, it was much different and much more significant than a polemic honoring battle dead. It was the most important political coup in our history. In three minutes, Lincoln made democracy the central premise of American Government. It is hard to overemphasize how daring Lincoln's words were. He insisted that the Civil War, the most divisive and bloody war in our history, be dedicated to the single idea that "all men are created equal." Lincoln insisted that government be "by the people." That meant in practical terms that blacks, then regarded in both north and south as subhuman, had to be treated the same as the rest of us in our system of government. Before Lincoln's speech, America had been a republic, but controlled by slave states. Lincoln moved it towards a democracy.

Lincoln's opponents knew the threat of Lincoln's words to their pre-civil war America. Four days after he spoke, the *Chicago Times* was saying, "how dare he,...standing on their graves, misstate the cause for which they died....to declare that Negros are their equals or entitled to equal privileges." Nevertheless, Lincoln's words prevailed.

Lincoln's philosophical and legal source was Jefferson's Declaration of Independence (perhaps the most significant political event of the eighteenth century in America) and its principle of the self-evident truth of equality. Jefferson's Declaration had been an indictment of the King of England to justify the American Revolution, but it was quickly put aside once the Revolution succeeded. Putting equality into practice would have meant an end to slavery, and America would not face that truth. Lincoln's few words brought it back to legal and political life.

After the Union's victory and Lincoln's assassination, Lincoln's Gettysburg Address compelled America to adopt the 13th, 14th, and 15th Amendments to the Constitution. Equality of all men, no matter what their color, became the legal norm, if not always the actual fact in the United States.

Following Lincoln's path, the Progressive movement in the early twentieth century expanded the concept of democracy with the 17th and 19th Amendments. Senators were required to be popularly elected, and women were given the vote. The tide of democracy then reached its limit in the 26th Amendment, spurred by the Vietnam War, requiring the states to lower their voting age to 18. Color, sex, and youth no longer were a bar to participation in American political life. The "people" meant everyone.

Democracy is still an often-used word today. However, it has become only a word. In reality things are quite different. The recent election furnished me with a few personal examples. Democratic lawyers spoke to me of suppressing the Republican vote in the hope of capturing the state legislature. I didn't ask "how do you do that," but it sure didn't sound like they were talking about driving voters to the polls. Republican lawyers sent a "task force" to Berks County to prevent "fraud." What kind of "fraud" were Berks County farmers, going to the polls, trying to pull off? Both groups' intent was obviously to intimidate people who were hoping to vote. Thirty years ago lawyers used to volunteer to work with non-partisan groups to make sure people weren't denied the right to vote. That's changed big time.

Our political process today does everything possible to ensure that people will not vote. In addition to my lawyer friends working on election day against voters they don't like, the whole election process consists of negative campaign advertisements designed to discourage anyone from believing a positive thing about any candidate. Why should anyone vote if everyone running is a jerk? Far more dollars voted in the 2002 election than people. The idea is to get only the most hardcore supporters that you want to vote for you to the polls. Otherwise, no one else is welcome. In Pennsylvania, news reports said the voter turnout was the worst in fifty years. The anti-democratic game plans of both parties are, unfortunately, working.

Lincoln thought differently. He trusted the common man, black or white, to do the right thing if allowed to join the democratic process. The Progressives trusted women the same way. In the 1970's, we did the same with young people. No one asked if these Americans would vote their way before inviting them into the democracy. Trust in human beings doing the right thing for the common good was the bedrock principle Lincoln put forth in his Gettysburg Address. We have lost that simple, but all-powerful trust in all people which Lincoln had when he spoke at Gettysburg. We need to get it back.

Two Mayors and a Lawyer

John Emerich Edward Acton
January, 2003

Lord Acton has always been a favorite of mine, so I thought he would come in handy to express some reservations about Bush and our foreign policy. I was surprised to get a favorable comment or two from Republicans. Perhaps that was the straw in the wind that the "old" Republicans were feeling more than a bit uncomfortable with the new southern axis of the party.

April may be the cruelest month, but January is clearly the biggest bore. The weather is predictably awful, and its only holidays, New Year's Day and Martin Luther King Day, come way too early or too late to be of any real comfort. And the worst thing about January is that February follows it.

January 10th, however, offers a marvelous opportunity to fix the problem. John Emerich Edward Acton's birthday was today in 1834. Now if you are of a liberal mindset that is something to celebrate.

Lord Acton published numerous articles, edited two journals, advised the great Liberal British Prime Minister William E. Gladstone, and founded the *Cambridge Modern History*. He was also the most controversial Roman Catholic layman of his day coming close to excommunication because of his attempts to reconcile his committed liberalism with his deep faith. However, Acton is remembered today for only one sentence, "Power tends to corrupt, and absolute power corrupts absolutely." That sentence could become the theme for a jolly old celebration of liberalism every January 10th.

If Acton was right, then we are headed for serious trouble in this world as America prepares to exercise its nearly absolute power in a war with Iraq. In their day, Acton and Gladstone fought a losing battle against the creation of a massive overseas British empire. That excess of British power left us stuck as a result with India v. Pakistan, South Africa, and, lest we forget, Iraq. As Michael Binyon noted recently in *The Times* of London, "the British Empire is now a black hole in history and few dare look into its depths."

Liberalism has gotten an undeserved bad rep in the last 30 years. It is hammered daily from the right as a worthless political creed which does nothing but tax and spend. Some American religious groups even see a liberal as synonymous with a libertine, i.e. someone who wants an immoral and sex-driven society.

However, Acton's liberalism was actually a middle ground flexible philosophy based on the middle class and its needs in a democratic and lawful society in the face of the mass politics of the industrialized left and an obscenely wealthy right. It favored government economy, but had the courage to recognize that a balanced budget includes limits on military spending even at the risk of claims that liberals are not patriots when they demand such a balance. It favored a flexible approach to the hot button issues of its day such as separation of church and state and education. Such flexibility might actually work today for similar tripwire issues such as gun control and stem cell research.

What is the point of Acton's liberalism today? Liberalism is anathema to both political parties. Republicans have not met a liberal they liked since 1872 when "Liberal Republicans" bolted from the GOP in the presidential election. Democrats fear the liberal label as lethal poison. The aversion which both parties have to liberalism is probably its greatest recommendation to the American people. With no political party holding it back, liberalism can afford to take stands on issues which the two political parties, clinging to their respective footholds, cannot do. Liberalism, with no political base, has nothing to lose.

Power is the coin of the realm in America today, and liberalism has fallen into complete disrepute. Pragmatism, which knows only the truth of success based on power, rules American thought. Acton's liberalism hoped for a world made safer and more peaceful by promoting morality rather than the raw rule of power. For instance, Acton hoped for an all-Ireland parliament in which both Protestants and Catholics would have full rights. That idea, together with the concept of a morally based foreign policy, was ridiculed at the time by hardheaded statesmen who believed in "realpolitik." Eventually, these "realists" helped bring on the First World War.

Today, a morally based foreign policy would translate into promoting, not trashing, treaties on disarmament and trying to develop an international consensus on issues like war crimes. In other words, liberalism could actually demand that America become part of a movement towards world law rather than world war.

So let's commit one day per year (perhaps January 10) to at least think about reviving those kinds of "liberal" ideas. Acton would have appreciated it.

Mark General Trexler's 150th Birthday with Celebration
April, 2003

Probably my proudest moment was my appointment by Lehigh County Court as one of the five Trexler Trustees. In 2003, we hit on the idea (Tom Christman our executive director was really the source of it) of a countywide year celebration of the General's birth. It was a tremendous success.

I once read a description of Harry Clay Trexler that portrayed him as something of a robber baron, one who made high profits out of the exploding new American economy, who sometimes exploited his own workers. I didn't agree with that characterization, but it is certainly a possible view of Trexler the man, because we know little about his life.

He left virtually no private papers, and the main impression of him comes from a collection of wonderful photos of the 1920s and early 1930s still hanging around Allentown. They show a short bulldog figure that looks like he was born to sit on his great white horse in a general's uniform. Or, he is a stocky fellow looking up at much taller men with a toothbrush white mustache. There are also great pictures of Trexler at the Game Preserve with some sad-looking Native Americans. Trexler must have been the most photographed Allentonian of his day, a testament to his significance here. From these pictures, one senses a man used to demanding and used to his commands being executed. He had strong, if not always politically correct, opinions.

We can also get something of "the man" from the corporations led and left behind – PPL, Lehigh Cement, and *The Morning Call*. Not much is left of his imprimatur on these once-local powerhouses.

A few legends persist. He personally paid the Army at Camp Crane (at the Fairgrounds) in 1917, until Congress found the money to properly do so. He secretly financed the desperate campaign of my grandfather, Malcolm W. Gross, to remain mayor in 1927 because "Mal" was a Democrat, and Trexler was the county's leading Republican. Out of cruelty, or in despair, he allowed small banks in Allentown to fail, saving the big ones during the Depression. However, those are only legends, and like the details of Trexler's life, they are fast fading, as those who have cherished them pass on. The truth is, we probably never will know much about Trexler as a man. However, we do know his legacy.

Most of us work all our lives to leave a legacy to our children, money being the most obvious means. But most of that kind of legacy ceases to be our own the minute we are gone, and it's commingled with our children's money. Trexler left a different legacy. Trexler's legacy lives for every one of us every day.

Seventy years after he died, it is impossible to mention Allentown's parks without mentioning Trexler. Our city's parks (13 percent of the city's total land) defined, invigorated, and in more recent years, sustained our city. The General, as head of the city's Planning Commission in the 1920s and 1930s, developed the concept of a city which would buy, own, and preserve land along the five streams that ran through it. That meant much more than parks for people in the new city. It made certain that the metropolis that grew up during Trexler's lifetime preserved an important part of the woods and streams, which had always been here.

Those parks were, and are, more than public playgrounds. They are living green space, reminding and challenging us daily not to waste the world of nature around us. More than just planning the parks, Trexler put his fortune behind his vision, contributing land and money during his lifetime and crowning the parks system with Trexler Park at his death.

Although childless himself, Trexler loved schoolchildren. At the start of the twentieth century, he underwrote Field Day, later called Romper Day, which brought the children of all the city's schools and summer playgrounds together for athletic contests and a good time. When I grew up in the 1950s, it still showed all of us that we were a community, that we needed to interact with each other even as we competed to be the best.

Finally, in addition to his land, Trexler left virtually everything he owned to us. As Kathryn Stephanoff pointed out when *The Morning Call* named Harry Trexler Philanthropist of the Century three years ago, "Philanthropy is difficult." Trexler overcame that difficulty by the totality of his generosity.

The Harry C. Trexler Trust has now given Lehigh County charities over $73 million since his death in 1933. The positive effect of those gifts is in our colleges, art organizations, and societies that take care of our children, seniors, and hospitals. Perhaps, more importantly, Trexler's legacy spawned a tradition of local giving, with similar trusts like the Century Fund, Pool Trust, Baker Foundation, and Gates Foundation. The personal generosity of Phil and Muriel Berman and Ed and Inez Donley, together with many others, combines with these foundations to create a powerful leverage with Trexler Funds to support those same charitable institutions.

April 2004 will mark the 150th anniversary of the General's birth in 1854. We all should use this coming year to remember and reinvigorate the General's legacy. With a yearlong celebration, our city parks could be revived and expanded. Trexler's concept of planning for preservation of land as a community grows could serve as a model for the rest of our county, if not the country. Our schools could again be used to unite us into a community in which we know and respect, rather than fear, those around us. And those thousands of charitable institutions that have benefited from the Trexler Trust and the many trusts it inspired could take a new look at themselves and Trexler's legacy as it benefits those they serve. Another ninety-six years of the legacy Trexler left us all in the new millennium – that would really be something.

Madison Proposed Seventeen Amendments
May, 2003

I wrote this piece for May Day. One of our Judges told me he had cut it out to use for future occasions. I hope it was of some use to him. The First Amendment and advocacy for it, for The Morning Call *and also for private citizens has literally made my career as a lawyer.*

James Madison proposed seventeen amendments. Congress eventually approved twelve. The states finally ratified ten. They are the first ten amendments to the Constitution, and they quickly became known as "The Bill of Rights." They were just as quickly forgotten because they applied only to rights against the Federal Government not the states. Until the Civil War, legal action occurred mostly in the state governments. States decided who was slave and free, who could own property (women mostly couldn't), and who could vote. The Federal Government did little but fight minor wars and govern Indian territories until they could become states.

One of Madison's rejected amendments would have made the rights, he spelled out apply to the states as well. However, that was too radical an idea and failed. It wasn't until 1868, with the Fourteenth Amendment, that the States were also made subject to the Bill of Rights. And it wasn't until the mid-twentieth century when the federal courts boldly began to apply the rights Madison gave us, that the Bill of Rights gained real meaning.

That meaning, like that of the Declaration of Independence, is pro-individual and anti-government. There is nothing subtle about it. The Bill of Rights is a radical concept. It is designed to be a thorn in the side of the beautiful structure which the Constitution itself set up, the Federal Government. It is not an accidental tension between government and vague rights. It is deliberate. The Bill of Rights weakens the strongest, and therefore, most dangerous elements in the government at its vital points by giving bunches of rights to us against our government.

The First Amendment protects the right of expression in speech, religion, press, assembly, and petition. Anti-war demonstrators in our streets and flags on our cars in support of our troops are lawful only because of it. It also seals government out of

117

our religious life. Madison felt more deeply about separating religion from the state than any of the other rights in his amendments. Today, however, the Bush administration's "faith based initiatives" call Madison's ideal into serious question, and may allow government money to corrupt these vital institutions.

The Fourth, Fifth, Sixth and Eighth Amendments give vital procedural rights against the government to the most hated (unless the press gets that prize,) and therefore, most needful of us — those charged with crimes. These amendments protect the unpopular against the powerful government weapons of double jeopardy, jail without bail, forced confessions, lack of counsel and secret trials by judges. They also protect against cruel and unusual punishments, which may include capital punishment or some of its forms. They mandate that today's judicial system at its core is one of justice for all, rather than a system whose first objective is to preserve the State. But crime is on the rise, and some argue that these rights seriously hamper the police in fighting it.

The Tenth Amendment protects states' rights against an otherwise all-powerful federal authority. Its limits are controversial today as a conservative Supreme Court breathes new life into our federal system. The Second Amendment may protect a state militia, or it may give gun owners themselves rights to their weapons. Which it does depends on which side of the gun control debate is exercising its rights under the First Amendment at a given moment.

Others like the Third and Ninth Amendments, taken with the whole body of the Bill Of Rights, reaffirm still developing and unclear rights like personal privacy. The limits of those rights, however, are being tested in the age of internet and anti-terrorism campaigns and have long been at issue in the abortion debate.

Finally, the Seventh Amendment preserves a right to jury trials in civil cases. It has been little used, but does reiterate how important the people's decisions are regarded even in our civil courts.

Today, as we try to decide these and other questions, which may determine our survival and will determine our shape as a society, we look to the Bill of Rights for help. It sends back a message that America was intended to be fundamentally just and equitable for all. How that message is translated into action in this new century is still being worked out.

One thing is certain. Madison and those who created our government feared it greatly. This is perhaps their greatest insight into what they accomplished. They could, as have so many of our politicians who have followed them, become enamored of their own brilliance and pushed their success in inventing a new republic beyond its own carefully constricted limits ending with a tyranny. Instead, they bequeathed us a limited government of checks and balances. They then went much farther. They set up a system of powerful rights outside our government and planted it in the Constitution. That was the genius of the first ten amendments which still are our Bill of Rights.

Alas, Poor Scranton, I Knew It Well

June, 2003

Scranton has always been near and dear to my heart. I lived there for a year when I clerked for Chief Justice Eagan on the Pennsylvania Supreme Court. Its Damon Runyon characters, its big city attitude, and its small town friendliness fascinated me and have stayed with me all the rest of my life. The piece was picked up and run by the Scranton papers as well. That was a nice compliment.

Alas, poor Scranton, I knew it well. I lived there in the 1960s in the "hill district" and came to love that town. Now Forbes, as reported in last Thursday's *Morning Call*, has put it third from the bottom on its list of best places for business and careers. Forbes' dump on Scranton is based on what appears to be topnotch research and statistics. And *The Morning Call's* story even had faint hint of gloating (or was it a sigh of relief) here because the Allentown-Bethlehem-Easton area comes out in about the middle of the 150 cities rated. So, poor Scranton looks to be on its last legs.

However, let's not celebrate our victory over Scranton too quickly. I still get to Scranton every few months, and my Scranton friends stay in touch by phone and letter. Scranton people are like that. They remember their friends. There is also much good in Scranton and much Allentown can learn from it.

Two governors, two auditors generals, a state treasurer, a lieutenant governor, an attorney general, and a chief Justice of the Supreme Court have come from Scranton since I lived there. Allentown gets a zero against that statistic. More importantly, three of those officials were Republicans, and three were Democrats. You see, politics is tribal in Scranton, fought with great glee by its citizens all year long rather than only on election day, which may explain why people vote in Scranton and don't here. However, once the fight is over, they stand behind their elected officials as a body encouraging and promoting them to run for high state office. As a result, politicians from Scranton aren't afraid to dream, and people in Scranton support their dreams.

Scranton itself seems alive when you drive into its downtown. Perhaps it's the University of Scranton, which proudly carries the city's name which has stretched itself right up to one side of the downtown with a modern attractive campus. Our colleges and universities ring the edges of Allentown as though afraid of the center city.

Take a look at Steamtown, a multimillion-dollar boondoggle if ever there was one, I thought when I first heard of it. Today it occupies 40 acres of the city's downtown with Boscov's department store and a large attractive mall next door. It brackets one side of Scranton's downtown with the University on the other. My Scranton friends tell me that it is the key to their new center city. Allentown's Lehigh Landing project has been on the drawing boards for several decades. It still is.

My friends tell me a lot about Scranton. They are clearly invested in their city. They generally love their town, know what's going on in it, and make it the centerpiece of their conversation. They live and breathe the good and bad times about their hometown. No one speaks that way about Allentown around here - if they speak about it at all. Scranton dominates ideas and activity in Lackawanna County. Allentown hasn't done that in Lehigh County since the late 1980s.

The difference may be in the two cities' role models. Scranton has always seen itself as a little New York - the greatest city in the world. Allentown has looked instead to Philadelphia — the butt of WC Fields' best joke.

So take heart Scranton, because you have a heart and a sense of community which Allentown somehow has lost. Forbes statistics don't tell the whole story. Forbes also has a top 10 list of smaller, towns, eight of which are located in North Dakota, South Dakota, Iowa, Kansas, and Arkansas — "America's Heart Land." On the whole, I'd rather be in Scranton.

President Bush Is Now on Record as Strongly in Favor of Marriage
August, 2003

Same sex marriage had become a major political issue as the 2004 presidential campaign neared. I wrote this to deflect the issue back to each state. However, the Republicans sensed an opportunity to get out the religious right vote in key states and as a result to put same sex marriage on the ballot in many states. The repetitive TV image of two women kissing after being married in San Francisco was a red flag in front of a Christian bull. The issue and the election went badly for the Democrats.

President Bush is now on record as strongly in favor of marriage. He wants marriage to be between men and women. He says his "lawyers are looking into the best way to do that." It seems "lawyers" have some use in Mr. Bush's world after all. For the past two and a half year we have heard about nothing but the bad "trial lawyers" who are destroying our legal system. However, these new unnamed lawyers are apparently different. They are looking into ways to "codify... one way or the other," the President's ideas on marriage. That may be a bit of a challenge for these lawyers whoever they are.

It seems to me this is not about marriage, but politics. Reading the Constitution, I can't find any provision that gives the Federal Government the power to regulate who marries whom. To make things even more difficult for Mr. Bush's legal team, there is a Bill of Rights. Specifically, the Tenth Amendment says that any power not granted to the Federal Government belongs to the states. That's the whole basis of the often heard Republican claim of "states' rights." Restricting state power over marriage and limiting who can marry whom means constricting the Bill of Rights. That has never happened before. On the contrary, the only changes in the Bill of Rights have been the expansion of people's rights in areas like voting rights for blacks, women, and young people. So it looks like Mr. Bush's ideas pretty much run afoul of both the Bill of Rights and the particular rights in the Tenth Amendment that his party has been using politically for more than fifty years.

Nor have the states been inactive in the area of marriage. On the contrary, there is probably more state legislation on marriage (including its dissolution by way of divorce) than any other topic. The Federal Courts have not only recognized marriage as a zone of state power, but Congress has already gone about as far as it can go into that zone by the 1996 Defense of Marriage Act which denies Federal benefits for single sex couples. That is why, as the Pennsylvania Dutch around here used to say, "it wondered me" why Mr. Bush spontaneously injected the subject of his strong belief in marriage into one of his very infrequent press conferences recently. Two reasons come to mind — both involve politics, not principle.

First, there is a perceived national crisis among Mr. Bush's all-important social right-wing base because of the Supreme Court's recent decision striking down a Texas law outlawing private gay sexual activity. That ruling prompted Republican Senate leader Bill Frist to suggest an amendment to the Constitution, so that states prohibiting single-sex marriage would not be forced to recognize those marriages if they were performed in other states. Apparently, Senator Frist and Mr. Bush fear that some state will adopt a single-sex marriage law, and as a result, other states will be required to recognize it by the courts under the Constitution's Full Faith and Credit clause. I don't think that is very likely, although it would be a boon to the beleaguered travel industry if masses of single-sex couples rushed to some far away state to marry, and then come back home to thumb their nose at local authorities.

Second, it is no coincidence that Mr. Bush took his stand just when the Vatican was issuing its own Defense of Marriage Act - a twelve-page position paper for government leaders opposing single-sex marriages. Mr. Bush split the Catholic vote exactly evenly in the 2000 election, but with his recent war in Iraq, he went against Pope John Paul's urging for a peaceful solution. At the time, the president was able to ignore the Pope because American Catholics thought that the war was a good idea. Now with things getting a bit out of hand in Baghdad, the White House needed to be on the same side of a major issue as the pontiff, and supporting marriage must have looked like the way to do that.

Let's hope I am right that the president's sudden need to promote marriage is strictly political because otherwise we are going to get into some dangerous legal territory. States can handle the marriage problem just fine. There is a civil side to marriage, including property rights, which is within their jurisdiction. There is also a spiritual side which belongs to the church. Each state and church can find where the line is drawn. We don't need to change the Tenth Amendment to keep them from doing so.

Two Mayors and a Lawyer

Gross' Folly
September, 2003

I stirred some anger in city hall with this piece.

Gross' Folly — that was what Allentown called the 2,100 acres of parks created in the two decades when my grandfather Malcolm W. Gross was serving four terms as Allentown's mayor in the 1920s and 1930s. Especially during the Great Depression in the 1930s, the parks ringing the city and hugging its five streams seemed a huge boondoggle. Even their final jewel, the Rose Garden, came in for bitter criticism immediately after it was completed — a waste of precious city tax money in hard times, they said. Its true cost had been covered up by the mayor, they said.

Today those same parks are Allentown's only assets unencumbered by negativism. Ask anyone from anywhere in the county, and you are almost guaranteed a positive response about Allentown's park system. People from the whole county actually come into Allentown to bike, picnic, walk, fish, and just mellow out in our parks. That's because there is nothing to compete with that mass of green beauty anywhere in the Lehigh Valley. Frankly, no one comes into Allentown for much of anything else.

Yet those same parks have been an asset hidden under a bushel by our city government for many years. The Trexler Trust, on which I sit, gives the city about 1.4 million dollars yearly to care for them, and that keeps them maintained. The city contributes a pitiful $885,000 for additional maintenance. Little or nothing is spent on capital improvements. At the same time, obsessed with security, our municipal government spends 25 million dollars of its annual budget on the police department alone. There is something wrong in our world when the best thing we have gets such an insignificant amount of our tax dollars and crime gets 25 million dollars. Is this discrepancy in city spending a reflection that crime and security have become that much more important in our lives than beauty and quality of life? I certainly hope that's not the case

Fortunately, there is glimmer of hope from the current administration that our parks are now, at least, on their radar screen. Challenged by an additional special grant of $500,000 from the Trexler Trust, the city will make a start next year towards recognizing that its park system is its most important asset. It has committed to hire a consultant to draw a plan for the parks' future and capital needs, and it will make modest capital improvements of its own as well.

Coupled with the idea of a real long-range plan and capital improvements, the city has begun dedicating a collection of small spaces in the heart of town for an Arts Park and other small passive green areas. Water spray parks are also in the works to give kids some fun in the summer heat. That's a creative expansion of a park system concept which, if pursued aggressively, can make Allentown center city something special.

Most importantly the administration will create a task force of citizens to help plan the parks' future and find out exactly who uses the parks. Once that happens we may be able to enlist the help of those people to make the parks a real selling point for Allentown and take some ownership in them.

That's a start, but there needs to be constant effort if Allentown is not to see its parks follow the city into a slow sad decline. We have to find the money, nerve, and energy to protect this vital part of Allentown even if it means risking our all.

When my grandfather was leaving office in 1939 after ten years of Depression gloom and the parks a bitter joke around town, he insisted the local press accompany him on a series of tours of the park system, thus giving it some favorable publicity for a change. He said you need to keep "hammering away" at a good idea. We need to start hammering again.

The Bill of Rights and the "Press"
November, 2003

I continued developing some of my ideas on the First Amendment, which I wrote for __The Morning Call__ forum on civil rights.

The butcher, baker, and candlestick maker get no special protection for their businesses under the Bill of Rights. The "Press," perhaps now the most unpopular business in America after lawyers, does. Why?

Well, first the founding fathers gave the itinerant printers, including Benjamin Franklin and pamphleteers like Thomas Paine, a great deal of the credit for igniting and sustaining our Revolution. John Peter Zenger was jailed in New York for his newspaper criticizing the British Governor's corruption, and then was dramatically acquitted and freed by his fellow citizens after a jury trial. Newspapers throughout the colonies pounded away on the theme of taxation without representation right up to the Declaration of Independence. That theme was one of the few things that united the original thirteen states.

During the Revolution itself, Paine's pamphlets "Common Sense" and "The Crisis" - "these are the times which try men's souls" — did as much to sustain morale as Washington's tiny army. The local newspaper or new pamphlet was looked on in those days as something worth protecting.

It was no surprise, therefore, that a constitutional protection against any federal law attempting to abridge freedom of the press was quickly written into the First Amendment in 1791. However, while everyone in the new republic was for a "free press," there was little thought given as to what the "press" was and how its "freedom" was to be protected. Apparently all that was originally meant by the First Amendment press clause was that the federal government could not institute a system of censorship before publication. After publication, even with the First Amendment, the printer still risked prosecution for libel, or as the Duke of Wellington put it, "publish and be damned."

For the most part, as Madison said, the press "protected by public opinion far exceeds the limits prescribed by ordinary rules of law." The press was actually so popular in the nineteenth century that Oliver Wendell Holmes, Sr. said the only thing Americans must have is their daily bread and daily paper. A free press didn't need the First Amendment; its popularity protected it from the government, and its often-biting criticism of authority acted as an important check on government power throughout our history.

By the 1960s, during America's struggle over segregation in the South, the press used its popularity to expose the brutal repression of blacks seeking equal rights to the whole nation. In order to stifle the bad news, southern government leaders hit upon arcane libel laws as a way of suppressing criticism. When an ad praising Martin Luther King, Jr. and criticizing local police appeared in the *New York Times*, Sullivan, police commissioner of Montgomery, Alabama, sued and won a $500,000 libel judgment despite the fact that he had been unable to prove any injury. Four libel suits demanding another two million dollars quickly followed against the *Times*. To stop them, the Supreme Court seized on the press clause to give unprecedented constitutional rights to the media. Thus, the First Amendment came to mean a great deal more than a bar on censorship. It now stood for the principle that the press, a private entity, was protected under the First Amendment, so as to function as a sort of private attorney general, checking government power and abuse. To help the press do that job, the Court required government officials and public figures to prove that the press knew its material was false before any damages could be awarded. It called that "breathing space."

The press eagerly took up its new expanded role in the 1970s, and pursued the government, exposing scandals like Watergate. Woodward and Bernstein became national heroes. Again, the Supreme Court granted the press another new constitutional right, this time access to the government and its records so that it could continue its efforts.

By the 1980s, however, fault lines had appeared in the whole concept of a privately-owned press checking the government. First, the print media engaged in excesses under the guise of "investigative reporting." In response to legitimate criticism of over-zealous reporters and the cost of defending lawsuits, newspapers backed off the practice and softened their criticism of the government at the same time. However, that retreat came at the price of softening government criticism. Second, television, always suspect as "the press" under the First Amendment, assumed a dominant role in our lives. Sixty-six percent of the public began getting their news from TV. By the 1990s, American households were bombarded with 50 or more channels showing graphic, repetitive images 24-hours per day. What was once called a wasteland often became a swamp. Unlike newspapers, TV is not just supported by advertising, it is often literally owned by its sponsors. In such an environment the problem becomes not the quality of news but separating news from hype.

The anomaly of a business depending on advertising, yet constitutionally protected, may be the ultimate test of the press clause in the 21st century. The government will always nibble at the edges of anything, like the press, which limits its power. That tension is manageable under our constitutional system. The real problem, however, is whether "the press," which now includes TV as its major component, can continue to act as a brake on government given its almost complete dependence on the billions of dollars of advertising from its government connected sponsors or whether it even cares to do so.

The government will always be with us. Will we also have a vibrant, independent press testing that government? The First Amendment's guarantee of a free press is a crucial brake on ever growing government power. The press, whether print or electronic, has to continue to vigorously apply that brake.

Two Mayors and a Lawyer

Who Was Walter Lippmann?
December, 2003

By now Iraq had become the core foreign policy issue of American politics. I had personally become obsessed with the daily reports of the war. Walter Lippman had always been a favorite writer of mine especially his work on religion and philosophy in the 1920s. I tried to use him to shift some of the discussion on the Iraq war to a more rational plane. I failed as both Iraq and Iraq politics got much worse.

Here's a one question pop quiz for those under 50. Who was Walter Lippmann? I will bet that unless you worked for a newspaper's editorial department, you didn't get that one right. Lippmann's career is a cautionary tale for those of us who write for these pages. No one even knows his name today, yet he was the foremost political columnist of his time. Successor to Henry Adams as a Washington pundit, confidant of presidents from Wilson to Nixon, his columns were so important that both Kennedy and the Russians leaked him information, which he then published to help defuse the Cuban missile crisis.

As a liberal in the 1920s, Lippmann promoted a new secular humanism as a moral substitute for what he saw as the failed religions of his day. By the 1930s, he had turned to Roman Catholicism and natural law as the only hope of strengthening the West's failing democracies against Nazism and Communism. However, it is the last years of his career which may still teach us something about our problems in Iraq. Lippmann tirelessly opposed the war in Vietnam, and Lyndon Johnson's escalation of that terrible conflict in the name of American security. Lippmann saw "security" as the other side of the coin of "empire." Security was then defined as a series of dominos with Vietnam being the first. If it fell, the argument went, the rest of Southeast Asia would quickly follow. Lippmann didn't believe that would happen, and feared a new American empire would arise in a distant ultimately indefensible Vietnam using security as an excuse.

Iraq is not Vietnam. We are infinitely more powerful now than then. Indeed as the world's only superpower, America is all-powerful. Still Lippmann's point about security and empire holds true today for the now bloody mess in Iraq.

We attacked Iraq as part of the new Bush doctrine of preventive war because we were told the nation's security interests were in imminent danger from Iraq's weapons of mass destruction. Security, we were also told, was so important that we needed to jettison fifty years of our European alliance to go it virtually alone against the terrible Iraqi danger. That all turned out to be wrong.

Now the administration tells us that even though we attacked for the wrong reasons, without our traditional allies, vital security interests require us to stay anyway. We can't leave, we are told, because to do so would give a victory to the dictatorship, which we just defeated. Thus, we now need to fight to give Iraq security. Donald Rumsfeld is saying we will need to be there at least until 2005. The *New York Times* reports a hundred thousand troops will be there in 2006. President Bush believes that Iraqi security will give America the security for which we attacked Iraq in the first place. However, he also told a British audience recently that there will be more wars like this one in order to give us peace and security. This is beginning to sound a bit like Lippmann's concern for empire.

Empires have a long history. That history includes cruel tyrannies, such as Persia and the Soviet Union, but also democracies like Athens and Great Britain. Empires' only common denominator throughout all of history is involuntary control of one nation by another for the controlling nation's own purposes. However, with that control inevitably comes responsibility. In Iraq, that responsibility will mean hundreds of billions of our dollars, and thousands of American soldiers dead or wounded all in the name of security, but really in the cause of an empire.

So the two sides of Lippmann's coin—security and empire—turn over in Iraq. In 1882, British Prime Minister Gladstone sent his troops into Egypt to protect British security there. Like President Bush, he said he was fighting a war "for love of peace." Sixty years after Gladstone, the British Empire was still in Egypt. Let's hope Lippmann's coin doesn't turn that often, for that long, in Iraq.

Trip through Ol' Dixie
January, 2004

I wrote this piece for Martin Luther King, Jr. Day. I knew only one black person growing up, so my trip south was quite a shock, not only because of the shabby treatment meted to African Americans, but also the sheer numbers of black people in the southern states. There were so many people being so badly treated just because of their status as blacks. It couldn't go on forever, but must have seemed like forever to all those generations living it.

In 1961 three fraternity brothers and I took our first trip through Ol' Dixie, driving nonstop from Allentown to Miami because we couldn't afford motels. I say "nonstop," but of course, we had to stop for gas. This is where I first encountered segregation.

The restrooms in South Carolina said "men," "women," and "colored" on their doors. That was very jarring to a Muhlenberg College junior. Not so much that the black people had to use a separate facility, I had heard about that, but that blacks were not "men" or "women," but a generic, sexless group of "colored." That one incident has always stayed with me. However, segregation by law made a whole race an underclass, and I can't begin to imagine what that was like, or the effect it had or still has on the millions of people of color who were made to conform to it.

When we reached central Florida, we blundered into a rundown "blacks only" gas station. The black attendant looked around fearfully before he quickly pumped a gallon or two of gas into our car. Segregation worked both ways. White people were to patronize white people's businesses. There was to be no risking of the mixing of the races on either side.

We forget, or gloss over, not just the evil of segregation, but that it was an evil embedded, encouraged, and systemized by American law — the law of the new Eden, the law of the symbol for the world of Democracy, the law of a great Western civilization. The small fines of segregation laws were only the superficial legal sanctions. The real penalty propping up segregation was death. The law winked at that real sanction and smirked at the deaths of thousands of blacks who were lynched (1,458 in one decade alone) because they dared to question their status. Slavery and segregation had the same root as the Holocaust; both made it legal and moral to systemize and engineer the persecution of a perceived "subhuman" race of human beings in what was supposed to be a modern civilized Western society.

In the beginning of the American republic, the law found a way to validate blacks' treatment as property. Since blacks were not really people, they could be owned like any other personal property. That nice legal fiction guaranteed the South's slave system, encouraged that system to expand into the nation's new territories and was the basis for the Fugitive Slave Law, ensuring any black who escaped into the North was returned to slavery. The Civil War was supposed to change all that, but after a brief period, slavery morphed into segregation, and American law again sanctioned that new face of slavery with the cruel hoax of "separate but equal."

Worse, in a way, the American value system glorified the good old racist South in films like "Birth of a Nation" and "Gone With the Wind." The Ku Klux Klan were the good guys upholding the old order against the mob of greedy darkies.

This whole charade was still going on when my friends and I drove south in the early 1960s, and it continued beyond then until Martin Luther King, Jr. came along a few years later. King undressed the American legal system along with our value system in two ways.

First, he dared to claim the same dream for black Americans as white Americans. Why, King asked, could not all Americans share the same dream of jobs, justice, and owning their own homes, instead of being required to dream separately? That idea was so simple and yet so unanswerable that it swept away two centuries of hypocrisy in the American value system.

Second, King put the law of segregation to the test of its own merits. Using mass politics, which bypassed the two major political parties, his followers peacefully violated and boycotted the law of segregation, but accepted the consequences of their actions by losing their jobs and going to jail. The law, and not King, broke in the face of that test.

Sensing their extinction was at hand, those who had so long profited from slavery and then by segregation, played the death card. King was murdered. But the truth that he forced on us would not die. We still owe Martin Luther King a great deal for those truths today, and we need to still guard them and promote them. And, as a lawyer, I thank him for freeing our law from two centuries of falsity.

When Does a Town Become a City?
February, 2004

I tried to put a positive spin on the vast change in Allentown with this piece.

In 1939, as he was leaving the mayor's office for the last time, my grandfather Malcolm W. Gross gave a series of interviews to the old *Evening Chronicle*. Among other things, Mal confided that at some earlier time he and other unnamed "city fathers" had plotted to drop the "town" from Allentown. The plot never came off, but the idea was that getting "town" out Allentown's name would send a signal locally, and nationally, that Allentown was now a city not a mere town.

Mal and the "city fathers" were right in one sense; Allentown's population had jumped from about 25,000 in 1910 to about 100,000 by 1939. That population growth meant that Allentown was a city as the dictionary defines the difference between a "town" and "city." A town is nothing more than a "defined area between a village and a city in size," and a city is just a "large town."

In much more important ways, however, the city fathers were wrong. Allentown was not a city in 1939. The real difference between towns and cities is that the town's citizens form a single community. The proof that was the case, in 1939, if nothing else, was that a group of city fathers even existed who could meet and speak for the entire community on a major issue such as Allentown's name. The fact that Allentown was one town would remain so for another 40 years. But it is not so today.

In the fragmented world of today's Allentown, no such group of city fathers exists or could exist. Allentown, regardless of population (and it is one of the few "cities" in Pennsylvania which is still growing in population), lacks the oneness of community that permitted it to function in the past. Today, with or without a name change, Allentown is at last a city.

Ironically, it is a city today at least in part by virtue of that loss of community. Its ethnic mix runs from Vietnamese to Lebanese to people from the Caribbean. It presents a full spectrum of color in the faces of its people. Spanish is heard on its main street as often as

English. Its neighborhoods, still neat and clean, exist independently of each other. Gone, forever, are the Elks Clubs, Labor Unions, Merchants Associations, and most significantly, a single high school that once linked those neighborhoods together.

Yet, this is typical of any city of any size in America. "City" in this country is a synonym for fragmentation of its people and communities. However, Allentown does have other tremendous assets as a city. Art museums, symphony orchestras, art schools, and smaller avant-garde art theaters and cultural groups exist here and nowhere else in the county. Three colleges and a large public library provide an educational component for the city. Three large hospitals and a major rehabilitation facility sit within the city's borders. A park system twice the size of New York's Central Park threads through the entire place. There is even a large athletic stadium (J. Birney Crum, not the proposed baseball field,) larger than anything like it in the county. These types of capital assets are impossible for any suburban community to duplicate.

So why isn't Allentown recognized as the interesting city it has become by the people living around it? It's because nobody from the suburbs goes there anymore. It's too crowded with people who aren't, well, suburban. Besides, there is nothing to do when you go there to drop off your child at the library or after one of those concerts. People who live in Allentown's suburbs either moved there from somewhere else and don't know that the entire city exists within a few minutes of them, or moved out of Allentown in the last two or three decades, and now mourn the town which they left, refusing to see the advantages of the city which has replaced it.

There must be a way to lure them back. How about food? Allentown already has a number of fine ethnic restaurants, but its diverse population could surely create more. Think of a cluster of Asian, Indian, Caribbean, and Mediterranean bistros, taverns, and eateries in downtown that you could hit before an art show or play. Think of a coffee shop where you could fire up some energy while you wait for a kid at an art lesson and think about whether that wouldn't attract those of us who don't live here anymore, to come back, and then enjoy the cultural and recreational assets which the city of Allentown can offer only if there is something else here as well.

Woodrow Wilson
March, 2004

Wilson has always been my favorite president. Even with his racist views he offered a third way to America between unilateralism and isolationism. It is a way we have seldom followed.

It's time to fess up and admit that when I was a teenager I wrote in a book. Defacing a book, my crime, has haunted me ever since. Worse, it was not just any book. It was volume 15 of *The Book of History*. I loved that series — every volume of it. However, in volume 15, I wrote, "history may prove me wrong but I believe Woodrow Wilson was the greatest president of the 20th century — 1957."

We don't hear much about Wilson today. President Bush did mention him somewhat favorably in a speech defending his invasion of Iraq last year, but that was in Great Britain, on the edge of old Europe, where the president's right-wing base seldom ventures. Republican columnists, in this paper, occasionally refer to "Wilsonian idealism," which I gather is something like "Massachusetts liberalism." Otherwise, Wilson has become a forgotten figure and a president certainly not mentioned by Democrats, who fear his idealism will be used against them.

Actually Woodrow Wilson was really quite an admirable, if ultimately tragic, president. Elected in 1912 as the first Democrat since Grover Cleveland twenty years before, Wilson was an unashamed liberal who quickly pushed legislation through Congress favoring free trade, established the federal reserve system, strengthened the anti-trust laws, created the Federal Trade Commission, and oversaw enactment of the 19th Amendment giving women the right to vote. Although Wilson's record on civil rights was poor, the rest of his domestic accomplishments were little short of sensational.

However, it's Wilson's contribution to America's role in the world that has forever defined him. In 1914, the whole world went to war — the whole world that is, except for the United States. Wilson, to use his successful 1916 reelection campaign slogan, "kept us out of war." By 1917, however, left with no choice because of Germany's indiscriminate sinking of our ships, Wilson brought America into

World War I. Americans were convinced he had done everything possible to avoid war, and that we were fighting not for ourselves but to "make the world safe for democracy." We went to war united largely because of Wilson's efforts.

A year and a half later with victory in hand, Wilson launched his final campaign to persuade us to join his new League of Nations. The League was a totally new approach to international affairs and America's position in the world. It called for international cooperation to preserve peace. It rejected the cynical balance of power that the British had used to preserve their empire for 250 years. Wilson's effort was a total failure; a series of strokes brought him down during a final speaking tour as he desperately tried to save the League from defeat in the Republican controlled Senate. Then, tragically, he lived as a crippled broken shell of a human being, clinging to the presidency and his concept of a new view of world affairs. As bitter and complete as his failure was, the right wing of the Republican party never forgot this rejected disdained figure who, it believed, symbolized woolly-headed internationalism. Wilson, even in defeat, had defined the fundamental question for America in the world. He saw the future world as a place where the strong used their might for right, not a place where the strong ruled regardless of right and considered only their own selfish interests.

The Bush administration has once again been confronted with the dilemma Wilson posed. In 1997, 150 countries signed a treaty banning the production, use, and sale of land mines and promised to destroy their stockpiles. Land mines kill not only in the war in which they are planted, but for generations afterwards, as that war's survivors try to remake their country. Recently, the Bush administration renounced the treaty's goals. Instead, it announced it would produce newer, safer, and more sophisticated land mines. It's hard to see how any land mine could be safe. Regardless, the administration's action smacks of the kind of unilateralism based on short-term selfish interests, which Wilson so hated and feared. The alternative of America joining and leading the world to destroy and ban land mines strikes me as a better, more Wilsonian course. And nothing that has happened since 1957 has led me to erase my note that Wilson was the greatest president in the last 100 years.

Activist Judges
April, 2004

Perhaps it was the 2004 election in which Janet and I were making a major effort for Kerry. Perhaps I was out of ideas on the local scene. For whatever reason, I shifted here to almost exclusively national and international issues in my columns.

Activist judges are responsible for many of the social controversies which currently bedevil America, according to President Bush. If those judges would only go away, so would these problems, he argues. As is his practice, Mr. Bush neither questions his own meaning nor allows others to do so. I was left, therefore, to look to other sources for a definition of activist judges. Since the President is famous for dividing every issue into black and white, I first tried to look at the opposite of activist judges to find his meaning. But the opposite of activist judges would be pacifist judges. The "war president" could not have wanted to be on the side of any pacifist.

In desperation, I turned to CNN's talking, or more accurately, shouting heads. Those shouting against activist judges gave me the answer. Activist judges are judges who interpret a state or federal constitution contrary to the will of the majority. In other words, they use the Constitution to protect some minority right.

If that definition is correct, the root of the problem was John Marshall, America's greatest Chief Justice. Marshall literally invented the concept that a judge has the power to interpret a constitution in ways that run contrary to the laws passed by Congress. Regardless of the wishes of the majority, judges can read a constitution to protect minority rights. Thomas Jefferson hated Marshall's idea. Jefferson hated Marshall as well. He even tried to impeach and remove a Supreme Court Justice who supported Marshall. Some years later, when Marshall continued to assert that judges had the power to say what a constitution means, even if it meant giving property rights to Native Americans, President Andrew Jackson is said to have remarked, "Marshall has made his decision; now let him enforce it." In the twentieth century FDR tried to pack the Supreme Court with five extra justices to out-vote its activist members who were interpreting the Constitution to invalidate his New Deal to protect minority business interests.

It is noteworthy that all of the aforementioned presidents were Democrats. In fair truth, the Democratic Party has consistently, throughout its history, championed the supremacy of the popular will over the power of judges to protect minority rights. It is also noteworthy that Americans have rejected the Democrats' arguments.

Alexis de Tocqueville, the Frenchman who best analyzed our democracy, observed that in America every political (i.e. social) issue ends up in court because the judges have the power to do something about it based on the Constitution. Tocqueville found this power to be fascinating for several reasons.

First, the power of American judges was unique. Elsewhere in the democratic world, the will of the majority, even if only temporary, was absolute. The only check on the majority's power was in a few aristocratic bodies such as Britain's House of Lords, but their members acted to protect only their own rights, not those of anyone else.

Second, the power to interpret the Constitution by judges is very limited because they can only decide the single case before them. They can strike down a law deemed unconstitutional, but not write a new one.

Third, and most important, the power of judges to interpret the constitution by reading it to protect minority rights actually preserves a democracy because a majority becomes an unchecked tyranny without it. The power of our judges to interpret our Constitution is what makes our Constitution meaningful. Otherwise, we would have no need for it. The legislature would simply decide our rights.

Mr. Bush should keep de Tocqueville's wisdom and the failure of his Democratic (he would say Democrat) predecessors in mind when next he takes on activist judges. After all we are all, part of a minority on some issue at some time in our lives.

The War Everyone Now Calls Simply "Iraq"
May, 2004

My obsession with the Iraq war continued, and it seemed it was everyone else's obsession as well. Here I worked in my longstanding belief in the First Amendment's right to gather news. Doonesbury, whom Janet had introduced me to, provided a new idea for a column on Iraq.

Some of the recent developments in the war everyone now calls simply "Iraq" involve coffins and cartoons. A contract worker working in Kuwait was fired because she sent pictures home of flag draped coffins she was paid to load onto cargo planes. A 1991 George H. W. Bush policy forbidding photographs of coffins returning from a war was the reason. Some historians claim the policy was created by George Sr. because he was angry at being shown on a split screen TV laughing at the same time as coffins were shown coming home from his Gulf War. Meanwhile, a newspaper in Colorado and a few others dropped the Doonesbury cartoon from their pages because it has been portraying battle scenes in Iraq in which one of its beloved characters B.D. had his leg blown off.

The reasons given for this censorship (that's what it is pure and simple) are privacy and taste. Not far below the surface of this justification, however, is the idea that it is vital to our troops' morale not to have anti-war sentiment develop here at home because we find out they are getting killed and wounded.

There is a long history of war photographs showing the reality of war. Some of the earliest were rows of dead soldiers on Civil War battlefields. Those photos were rushed to New York and caused a sensation when they were displayed in the city's store windows. Photos of the dead in trenches and hanging on barbed wire in World War I defined the horror of the "Western Front." Yet our soldiers in both conflicts fought on to victory.

Oddly, much the same can be said about cartoons from earlier wars, which invariably showed unshaven, cigarette smoking G.I.'s, cracking jokes about bad chow or stuffy officers. They looked ragged, but they fought nonetheless.

143

The stark reality of the camera and deliberate exaggeration of cartoon characters each told us Americans the truth about the sacrifice, pain, and brutality of the war men and women were fighting to create the legends and glory of war for future generations.

Not so Iraq. This has been a "feel good" war from the get go. Before it started, and even now, the costs were never an issue. Those supporting this new crusade (that's what this moralistic war is) could never tell us how many tens of billions it would cost. Besides, they said we would not really be paying for it because Iraqi oil would cover the costs. If the oil money weren't sufficient, we would just borrow the money. More important, we didn't have any estimate of how many of our people would be killed or wounded. As they got killed and wounded from week to week, we were told it was only "terrorists" in a few hot spots doing the killing, and the rest of the place was improving rapidly. Last week, Democratic Senator Joe Lieberman described how well things were going. More Iraqis had jobs—there's a lot of work for guards and police, for instance. The true number of troops wounded like B.D. has never been given to us either. The military "estimates" run from 3,000 to over 4,000. Nor are the numbers of civilians killed even of interest to the military. Apparently, it doesn't count them. The blood and horror of war weren't really happening, according to the people running the show.

Then I saw flag draped coffins on that illegal photograph. The image composition was stunningly beautiful – perfect lines of boxes, perfect geometry with the flags and magnificent colors. After that first effect, there was a second wave of terrible sadness, realizing that perfect symmetry hid dead men and women. The same kind of emotion hit me when I saw that cartoon of B.D. lying in a hospital bed with one leg. The reality of photos and the obvious unreality of cartoons somehow give us a truth, which our leaders do not. Truth is not so much anti-war as understanding that William Tecumseh Sherman was right when he said, "war is hell." We need to realize that before we start more "feel good" wars.

Thomas Jefferson and "The Pursuit of Happiness"
July, 2004

You will note if you have read this far that I wrote often about history around holidays. Here I wrote on the Declaration of Independence and the odd words "pursuit of happiness" which Jefferson used, and the Americans have quoted for centuries never being quite sure what they meant.

As a confirmed pessimist, it has always troubled me why Thomas Jefferson put the "inalienable" right to "the pursuit of happiness" in the Declaration of Independence. It seemed to me that the government had no business in the happiness business. I recognize the Declaration only gave us a right to pursue happiness, but even that I thought was dangerous, because I've always equated happiness with loss of self-control. What could Jefferson have been thinking?

Apparently what he had in mind was what the eighteenth century called "public" happiness, meaning a people's right to its own land and to fill that land with its progeny. Independence was synonymous with these concepts. Private happiness, or hedonism, was not what Jefferson was talking about, thank goodness. Old Europe (and it really was old Europe in the 1700s) monarchs didn't believe in public happiness. In fact, their taxes were so high, arbitrary, and inequitable, that an Italian Jesuit named Muratori wrote that a prince should only have his tax collectors, "sheer the flock, not skin it." Now those were real taxes.

A Frenchman named Chastellux, (those darn French keep popping up in our history) had identified three great evils which government used to stifle happiness — slavery, superstition (by which he meant Roman Catholicism), and war. Jefferson had read Chastellux and saw all three of those evils as lethal to public happiness.

Jefferson's concern that government gives its people a chance to enjoy public happiness caused him to include its pursuit as one of the basic rights our government was specifically charged to secure in the Declaration. Life and liberty were the other two.

The idea that Americans should pursue happiness (or some would say independence), and that the government promote that pursuit became central to their psyche. For more than a hundred years after Jefferson wrote the Declaration in 1776, Americans charged west, encouraged by free government land. Happiness was just over the next mountain range. The frontier myth, as historian Frederick Jackson Turner pointed out, was at the core of American thought. Then in 1890, the frontier officially vanished when the Census Bureau said it could no longer find one. The United States truly reached from coast to coast. There was, of course, a dark side to America's pursuit of happiness. The yearly march west of the frontier also marked the mile-by-mile extermination of the Native American civilization. Without a frontier there was no happiness to pursue.

Then a new happiness, the automobile, almost immediately replaced the frontier. In 1903, Horatio Nelson Jackson became the first person to drive across the country. Perhaps symbolically, Jackson drove west to east. Unlike the railroad or the ocean steamer which controlled where you went and when you went, the automobile answered its driver's command. The open road, seemingly endless, gave birth to a new happiness to pursue. Americans drove for the sake of driving, took rides in their cars around the block, enjoyed the USA in their Chevrolet. If Americans couldn't live off the land, as Jefferson hoped, they could at least see it from their car windows.

The government again did all it could to secure the new happiness. Cities paved streets, and then states built roads. Pennsylvania built the first turnpike in the 1930s. There was no speed limit to interfere with the pursuit of drivers' happiness on the new Pike, at least until drivers started killing themselves.

Every effort was made to keep Americans in their cars. If there were break-ins, automatic door locks were developed. If people were killed in accidents, air bags were installed.

Like the frontier, however, the myth, which married the auto to happiness, is coming to an end. Independence as symbolized by our car has become dependence on foreign oil. The president of Exxon said recently we would now always be dependent on Mid-East crude. The self-service gasoline pump forces us to see this fact. Every week, we jam the nozzle into our car, like a drug addict does a needle in his arm, and watch the dials spin. There goes any happiness before we even get on the road. Then we fight our way into traffic, merge, stop for a red light, construction, etc., etc. The open road is gone and the government only wants to move us along happy or not.

So with America's second myth of happiness slipping away, can we find a new one? Perhaps, the Internet certainly has that possibility. It is not taxed, it is seemingly unlimited, and it is available, at least in theory, to all. We'll see if it also gives enough sense of independence to make us pursue it for another century.

Kennedy and the 1960 Election
July, 2004

More on politics and church politics.

A friend of mine said recently that in the 1960 election people were afraid Kennedy would listen to the Pope if he won, and that this year, they are afraid Kerry won't. Religion is back in politics. A recent poll showed over 40% of Americans think that's a good idea. That's up 20% over a few years ago.

The use of religion in the Kennedy election was nothing new. In 1840, when the Whigs nominated William Henry Harrison ("Tippecanoe and Tyler too,") they met in Harrisburg and used a church for their convention. In 1884, the Republicans lost New York and the presidency when a speaker called the Democrats the party of "Rum, Romanism, and Rebellion." That outraged the Roman Catholic vote, which went to Grover Cleveland. The speaker was a Protestant minister. In 1913, Woodrow Wilson was attacked as being "offensive to the Catholic church" for a patronage appointment. The attacker was the Archbishop of Boston. *Barron's*, the financial journal, recently reported that during his June visit, President Bush asked Pope John Paul II to push the American bishops to raise the abortion issue during this fall's election. And of course, we have all seen Pat Robertson's TV operation.

Religion is and always has been a big part of American politics, like it or not. However, it is quite different when religion becomes part of government. That brings the First Amendment into play.

The First Amendment bars two separate government activities relating to religion — "free exercise" and "establishment." The free exercise clause prevents the state from interfering with our religious practices. It comes up mostly in fringe situations such as the recent one where an atheist father, who didn't have custody of his child, objected to her saying "under God" when she recited the Pledge of Allegiance in public school. The Supreme Court, quite rightly, tossed his case because he lacked standing to bring it in the first place, but not before Attorney General Ashcroft had a chance to outgrandstand the dad by slamming the lower court decision. Problems with the free exercise clause almost always arise when rituals like the Pledge offend someone. We would do better to worry about whether our children have any idea what they are pledging, and let the courts decide free exercise claims on a case-by-case basis.

The establishment clause in the First Amendment is another story. James Madison, who wrote the Amendment, hated an established church. He had much experience with that odious concept in his native South where citizens were taxed (the forced tithe) to support the unpopular English/Anglican church. Madison feared an established church could lead to a church government partnership like those which already existed in the Catholic countries on the European continent.

There's no longer any real danger of church state partnership in America. There is, however, a growing trend of religious groups tapping into the public till. The government debt is now so huge that a few millions more to this or that religious institution will barely be noticed. That's part of the problem, but the real danger is not to the already overextended public purse. It is that when religions take public money, they become so enmeshed with government that they lose their independence.

It was not the First Amendment's intent to strengthen religion by separating it as completely as possible from government. However, that unintended consequence is one of the Constitution's great achievements. American religion today is stronger because we freely choose to support it. Government support of religion, whether it is called faith-based initiatives, vouchers, or something else, ultimately deprives religion of its ability to independently function. Religions then become government owned religions, not our religions.

Bomb Squads, Barbed Wire, and Troops
September, 2004

Janet and I went to Boston for the Kerry convention. We met some fun people. I came home inspired to work for the "cause". It turned out to be a lost "cause."

Bomb squads, barbed wire, and troops with heavy weapons—they were all there; the hard zone which can only be accessed with multiple credentials, IDs, and metal detectors, closed highways and residents fleeing their homes. They were there, too. Baghdad? No, Boston and New York for the Democratic and Republican Conventions.

The media event, which is what national political conventions are today, has, at the cost of hundreds of millions of dollars, met the war on terror. Both survived. Whether the national political convention itself should as well is a different question.

For much of our history the nominating conventions, acting as the vehicles for choosing each party's candidate for president, have played an important part in the slow and still incomplete movement towards popular choice in our political system.

Conventions, which have a reputation for the smoke filled room in which dark horses like Franklin Pierce and Warren Harding were picked by party bosses, actually were an important step toward democracy. Andrew Jackson imposed the idea on the Democrats in 1832. Before then, each party's presidential candidate was chosen by a caucus of their congressmen in Washington. Jackson hated the elitist "King Caucus" and favored a national gathering of the whole party. As a result, the first Democratic Party convention was held in Baltimore. Not surprisingly, the Democrats re-nominated Andrew Jackson for another term.

Thereafter, party conventions did rather well in picking our leaders. Lincoln, Cleveland, Wilson, Franklin D. Roosevelt, Truman, and Eisenhower were all nominated at hotly contested party conventions. However, by 1960, the convention system for selecting candidates was effectively finished. Two things happened that year. Kennedy won 16 straight state primary elections and made it impossible for the Democrats not to nominate him, and TV became totally dominant in our political system.

Since 1960, conventions have little or nothing to do with selecting candidates for president. Instead, a crazy quilt of state primaries knocks out contenders one by one. Money (or lack of it actually) and TV decide the winner long before the summer conclaves. Party conventions are now simply an attempt to showcase politicians looking as good as possible to the national TV audience. Nothing could better demonstrate this than the statistic that 15,000 media people attended this year's Democratic Convention to cover only about 4,000 delegates.

Party platforms remained controversial for a time. In 1964, for instance, the Democratic Freedom Party forced the Democrats to adopt a plank which led to the Civil Rights Act of 1965. However, platform fights, too, have long since faded.

Had nature taken its course, the national convention would have long since gone the way of the dodo bird. It would have been replaced by some form of national primary.

However, the parties, not wanting to give up free TV time, keep holding conventions and have turned them into a sort of a coronation married to an infomercial in which everything is tightly choreographed. As Russ Schriefer G.O.P. convention program director said, "we're taking lessons from TV shows." The platform is still adopted, but no one reads it. A keynote speech is still given, but it and all other speakers are strictly controlled for time, tone, and content. At least Al Sharpton raised his voice at the Democratic Convention.

Two ironies have nevertheless intruded into these TV packages. First having at last wrung every ounce of spontaneity out of the party conventions, the networks decided that lack of interest required that broadcast coverage be limited to an hour per night. Not mentioned in the networks' decision was that they would have lost ad revenue from their vapid regular programming by showing the conventions. Second, the fear of terror attacks made the conventions so "safe," no one could simply go and watch them in person.

Nobody goes there anymore; it's too safe. Gone are the galleries chanting, "We want Wilkie" (Philadelphia 1940). Gone are the demonstrators outside the hall (barbed wire takes care of them now) and the demonstrators inside the hall marching down the aisles waving their standards. Instead, delegates sat politely and raised color-coordinated signs on cue.

As with most of our major national and international events, the Super Bowl and even the Olympics, it doesn't matter what the event is supposed to mean to the institution holding it. It matters what the event looks like on television. How long can the institutions which once held these events for a real purpose, meaningful to them, and their members survive if their events have become so purposeless?

Lehigh Valley democratic Congressman Fred. B. Rooney with Attorney Malcolm Gross in Washington, D. C. during his close, but ultimately unsuccessful campaign for district attorney in 1971. Gross, thirty at the time was one of the youngest lawyers to seek that office. Congressman Rooney was an ally and close supporter. He invited Gross to Washington, D. C. for various campaign events.

To Be Remembered after Your Own Generation
October, 2004

Another piece on General Trexler and the unfolding celebration the Trustees, staff and volunteers put on for his 150th.

To be remembered after your own generation passes away is unusual. To be remembered fondly is almost unheard of. On October 10th all of us will celebrate "Harry's Day in the Parks" in the Allentown's Park System, and remember very fondly that this is the 150th Anniversary of General Harry Clay Trexler's birth.

This free public celebration is an opportunity to showcase the beautiful Allentown Park System. Many different activities will take place in Allentown's parks that day. From 11 am until 5 pm, residents of the city of Allentown and Lehigh County will participate in scavenger hunts, fishing demonstrations, and games and hands-on projects for children. In addition, concert performances, ethnic dancing, nature talks, and at 5 pm an Interfaith Service will be conducted. The "General" would have loved it.

Much has been written and said during this yearlong celebration of Trexler's birth. His contributions to this community were immense and continue today and beyond in the form of the Trexler Trust benefiting all of us. However, nothing in all of that matches the Allentown Park System, which Trexler promoted during his long life and stimulated after his death in 1933 by the handsome gift of Trexler Park to the City as a "public park." Trexler's promotion of the parks is a lesson for us on how to make an idea come alive, move ahead, and continue to have great meaning for a community decades later.

First, Trexler used his official position as head of the city planning commission and his unofficial position as Allentown's leading and wealthiest citizen to constantly push city government to acquire parkland. Then he did much more because he pushed the city to spend the money necessary to make the land useful to its citizens.

Second, Trexler put his money where his mouth was. From the beginning of his campaign for public parks, when he took responsibility for West Park (Allentown's first park) in 1908, until his death when he gifted Trexler Park to Allentown, Trexler was there

155

with his own funds, to get things started. He followed all of that up with the Trexler Trust, which now gives the city about 1.5 million dollars each year to improve and maintain those parks.

Finally, Trexler made public parks an idea something other people wanted to be associated with. He used his skills as an entrepreneur when he assembled groups of businessmen to support his project to gather support for public parks in Allentown. It became the thing to do to support a great park system. Today, we see this as obvious. It was not at the time. The new Allentown, which was exploding with population growth in the twenty odd years from 1910 to 1933 when Trexler was prominent, like all growing communities, was a raw place growing too fast, and not really concerned where that growth was leading it.

Trexler and his lumber company had been part of that rapid and often disruptive growth. Trexler's company stripped the green mountains all over Pennsylvania to supply the lumber, which, while making his fortune, made that growth possible as well. However, at some point, as his wealth and fame became enough, he launched himself into a new career no longer as Allentown's leading citizen, but as its leading public citizen. The centerpiece of his public spiritedness was the city's parks.

It has been a wonderful year as we shared and enjoyed the legacy of General Harry Trexler, however it would be incomplete without Harry's Day, October 10th.

It Is Time for Another True Confession
October, 2004

I guess I was ahead of my time with my concerns about the national debt and the weakening economy.

It is time for another true confession. I got a D in Economics 101. What Thomas Carlyle called the "dismal science" has always been beyond me. I could never get the lines to meet on those graphs representing supply and demand.

After college, I hit on a way of avoiding economic thinking. I paid my bills every month. Since I didn't owe anyone, I didn't have to worry about economics, which is really all about debt, or more exactly, about money we don't have, but hope we will have some day, so we can pay debts we have now.

However, I am a born worrier. Not having to worry about my own debts, I began worrying about the national debt. It has gone up, in case you missed it, by about a trillion dollars in the last four years. That's 12 zeros or double that number of zeros if you add another trillion for the next four years according to the congressional budget office. A good part of those zeros are caused by the war in Iraq. I don't like zeros. We used to call losers "real zeros," and there is something scary about zeros.

Nevertheless, I was immediately reassured by two people who really know economics — Professor Allen Greenspan, who has written whole books on the subject, and President Bush, who has an MBA from Harvard. Don't worry, they said, that two trillion is not nearly as great a percent of the Gross National Product as the great Ronald Reagan ran up when he was president. Okay, that was comforting to my fevered brain, but then I thought the debt still had to be paid back some day like I would have to pay my bills. You don't understand, the Prof and Prez, said, the government can just print more money to pay it off. You can't do that with your own debts.

Print more money. That brought to mind a time I was in Portugal 30 or so years ago. They had money there they called the escudo. Portugal owed a big national debt (mostly to pay for a bad war in a faraway country,) so they just printed more escudos to pay for it. Anyway, when I got there the escudo was worth .05 of a dollar and when I left, two weeks later, it was worth about .03 of a dollar. More of those frightening zeros, and this time on the wrong side of the decimal point. Not a good thing I thought - but I don't understand economics.

Then my worried mind stumbled onto the trade deficit. It's running about 700 billion dollars per year. That's 11 more zeros every year for the stuff we are shipping in here, which doesn't equal the stuff we are shipping out there. Once again the Prof and the Prez soothed me. Don't worry they said, every month people buy U.S. Treasury Bonds to cover that 700 billion per year. So Americans are showing how much confidence they have in our government by buying a slice of it just like they did during World War II. That's great. Not quite, the Prof and the Prez said; it's the Chinese and Japanese who are buying those bonds. Some guys in the Tokyo geisha houses and forbidden city in Beijing decide every month how much of America they want to buy, and that makes up for all those zeros in the trade deficit. What happens if they decide to sell America some month? Don't worry, said the Prof and Prez, we'll pay them with cheap dollars by just printing more money. We have already made the buck worth about 20% less than it was 2 years ago, and we are driving it down more all the time.

Finally reassured that our economics were in good hands with the Prof and Prez, I relaxed. Then one more worrisome thought fleeted across my mind. It was of old movies I'd seen of Germans in the 1920s. Their government paid for a war by running up a big national debt and printed lots of money to cover it. The Germans were pushing wheelbarrows to the store full of their new money to buy a loaf of bread. Don't worry, said the Prof and the Prez, the Americans now own pickups and SUVs. They have a lot more room in them to hold money.

Taking Down the Invisible Fence
October, 2004

The Human Relations Commission asked me to give a speech at its annual dinner. It went over well and The Call *reprinted a version here. My main point was that the fencing off of the city's black and brown population from the suburbs by an invisible economic fence was immoral. Religious leaders needed to say so as they had about segregation. The speech was well received, but I never saw any evidence that the idea got through to the suburbs where it was aimed.*

This article is adapted from the keynote address given by Allentown Attorney Malcolm J. Gross at the Allentown Human Relations Commission dinner on Oct. 14th. He addressed the 50th anniversary of the Brown vs. Board of Education *case in which the U.S. Supreme Court ruled against segregation in public schools, and the 40th anniversary of the commission.*

In addition to hearing a good deal about *Brown* this year, we have also heard a bit about activist judges, particularly in Massachusetts. There is concern, no, actually alarm, in some quarters about the harm these judges do by making decisions interpreting their states' constitutions. I thought that is what judges were supposed to do – read their states' constitutions and protect fundamental rights against the tyranny of occasional majorities.

Regardless, Massachusetts apparently has a long history of this kind of activist judicial behavior. In 1783, that's five years before there was a U.S. Constitution, the Massachusetts Supreme Court declared slavery violated the state constitution. It said, "There can be no such thing as perpetual servitude of a rational creature." As a result, the first national census in 1790 recorded not a single slave in Massachusetts.

However, Massachusetts history is not all positive thereafter. In 1850, nearly 70 years later, Harvard Medical School admitted its first three black students (all men, by the way) with one white woman, apparently for a good measure. Then it expelled them all a semester later because the white male student body was so offended that it threatened to transfer to Yale. Massachusetts would not tolerate slavery, but it also would not give equality of opportunity to those it freed.

Unfortunately, America followed the same pattern. It abolished slavery with the 13th Amendment in 1865, but then used a cruel legal fiction (separate but equal) pretending its races could somehow live equal and yet separate. In 1954, The U.S. Supreme Court finally changed that in the case of *Brown vs. Board of Education*. It had taken ninety-one years for any congress, president, or a court to face the seemingly obvious wrong of segregation. Finally, to its great and everlasting credit, when all those failures were undeniable, the Supreme Court, at last, did act and act decisively, and perhaps as importantly, unanimously, in *Brown*.

Other courts mostly decide only winners and losers in the matters before them. The decisions in those other courts have great meaning to the parties, but no meaning beyond those parties' own interests. When the Supreme Court speaks, it does something more.

In Supreme Court cases, of course, there is also a winner and loser. There were real winners in *Brown,* and those people are often forgotten. It was a group of children in five states whose families suffered terribly for the supposed great sin of making America look at itself.

The victory won by those children and others like them was an ugly victory. By day, white mobs barred the schoolhouses, which the court had opened, and by night, white-hooded men burned churches. But though ugly, it was not bitter. Those children who were the winners in *Brown* had no doubt that they had won – and the mobs knew they had lost.

Which brings me to the second, more unusual, effect of a Supreme Court decision; it is a national precedent, a building block binding for all courts throughout the nation in all their future decisions. *Brown* was that, and by the legal logic of equality, regardless of status flowing from it, caused decisions requiring that same equality before the law in everything from the criminal courts to the voting booth. The entire American legal system was thus changed forever by *Brown*.

There is also a rare third consequence of some Supreme Court decisions, but only a few great ones. Those great decisions work a philosophical and moral, as well as legal, change in our country. *Brown* was one of those few cases.

It forced us, and inspired us to look at the way we were conducting our individual and collective lives. Because of *Brown*, the simple but hard question had to be asked – were we discriminating against other Americans? Had we, as had Massachusetts in 1850, declared a people free and then denied them the opportunity of freedom? It takes a while for those kinds of challenges to percolate down to the local level, but finally they do.

They hit Allentown in 1963. My father, Jack Gross, was mayor then and very popular and about to start a second term. It seemed he could do no wrong – people even praised him for the way he raised their taxes. Much was going on. The city was literally throbbing with life and activity. It had celebrated its bicentennial with a massive parade – more than 100,000. It was named an All-American City.

As something of an afterthought, my father had also pushed through the City Council an ordinance creating the Human Relations Commission during that time. I don't know where he got the idea for a commission to promote equality. At home, he never spoke of it. He did appoint his close friend and political ally, former *Morning Call* reporter Charles Ettinger, as its first chairman, so the idea may have come from Charlie. Regardless, the commission would not have happened without the Supreme Court's powerful statements on equality in *Brown*.

My father then also appointed a group of community leaders as its first members. That was typical of his governing style, and it gave the commission instant credibility. Later, that was to play a critical role in helping in a crisis in Allentown.

At the time, however, I believe he probably thought of the commission as simply another good idea. But it certainly wasn't a high priority for him, and he warned its members to be cautious about their actions because the council controlled their budget. There was a lesson there for future commissioners as well.

Anyway, my dad's principle goal for 1964 was a massive redevelopment project for the center city area, which today includes City Hall, the Allentown Manor, and upscale housing on S. Fourth Street. In order to pull that off, he had re-energized the Redevelopment Authority and had gotten federal and state funds for the project. There was, however, a final hurdle. People lived in the area where all this was supposed to happen. Not surprisingly, since the area had been declared blighted, many of those people were poor and black.

That meant that the whole redevelopment project was stopped dead unless new housing was found for those people. Sadly, and I think we now know, wrongly, no consideration was given to the fact that there were real neighborhoods in those blighted areas which functioned and struggled, but kept the communities together.

I suspect that my father's almost desperate (he had only a short time to live and he knew it) drive to get the redevelopment project done is what made him take up the cause of public housing. Or, it may have been that because he basically was a very good and decent man, he simply believed something had to be done for people who were going to lose their homes because of his project. Or, it may have been the first reason that opened his eyes to the second. Regardless, he became a champion for Allentown public housing.

It cost him personally and politically. For the first time in Allentown history there was a bitter, and I must say, bigotry-based campaign on a public issue. My father's car was egged, large bugs were let loose in our home, we got hate mail, etc., etc. Council meetings became a mob scene. Those things just didn't happen in Allentown – not then anyway.

My father fought back; he held council together on its decision to approve the public housing project that would become Cumberland Gardens. He drove the paperwork for it through Harrisburg and Washington at amazing speed. But, it was still touch-and-go whether new public housing would be built.

Then he got support from the Human Relations Commission. The commission, in its first significant public act, issued a detailed fact-finding report that supported the need for public housing at the Cumberland Gardens site. Its facts were unanswerable by public housing opponents. Facts are stubborn things, even when faced by bigoted rhetoric. Facts, coming from a respected organization like the commission, still meant something in Allentown.

But, something else happened as well. Individual members of the commission spoke up forcefully against what was happening to the All-America City. Those members, whom my dad had appointed, were the priests, ministers, and rabbis of Allentown's religious community. That stemmed the tide of hatred. Cumberland Gardens was built.

Brown vs. Board of Education proves that when the Supreme Court speaks on a moral issue liked discrimination, Americans listen, and eventually, they act, even in the face of nasty, racially motivated opposition. They did in Allentown in 1964 – not quickly or easily, but they did. *Brown vs. Board of Education* spawned the commission, but its success and Allentown's success, in at least providing some housing for some of its poor, would not have been possible had it not been that our religious leaders spoke out against discrimination when it counted.

Allentown needs that kind of help again today. Almost all people of color in this county live behind an invisible political fence in Allentown, which runs along the city line. Almost all the poor in Lehigh County live behind the same fence. Almost all poor children of color in this county attend schools in Allentown behind the same fence. The solution to this disgraceful violation of America's principles of equal treatment is obvious. The political boundary lines that define that invisible fence must be erased to give us all ownership of the situation.

Unfortunately, while the solution is obvious, it has little hope of adoption. Power for that kind of change lies exclusively with those in our state government who will not allow it. Meanwhile, outside that fence in the suburbs where everyone else lives and works, now stand many of the religious institutions, which in the 1960s were a vital part of Allentown. They have followed their white congregations out of town. It is the clergy of those now-suburban religious institutions who need to look to the example set by their predecessors in Allentown during the public housing crisis in 1964. The politicians will not act. The courts have done their all.

Thus, there remain only our religious leaders. It is up to them to speak, speak often, and speak forcefully against the kind of de facto segregation which today exists in this city and this city's schools. It is up to them to demand that some way be found to end the immoral inequality, which has crept around the change in American life initiated by *Brown*.

If that occurs, if the moral side of *Brown* is again brought front and center in our suburbs by those charged with our moral leadership, as it was in our city in 1964, the rest may follow.

Two Mayors and a Lawyer

Evangelicalism and Politics
November, 2004

The Scopes trial and Clarence Darrow have always fascinated me. Darrow was one of the reasons I went to law school. Here I had a chance to link Scopes to liberalism's political failure in America. I got the idea from Garry Wills.

Billboards supporting President Bush in the recent election here proclaimed "one nation <u>under</u> God." The billboards emphasize "<u>under</u>" for good measure. When did God start to vote Republican? The answer to that question, at least for American evangelicals, seems to be July 1925. That was the date that American liberalism divorced Protestant evangelicalism. It happened at the John Scopes trial in Dayton, Tennessee. The "monkey trial" was over a vague Tennessee law barring teaching evolution as science.

Until the Scopes trial, American evangelicalism had a history of liberalism or even radicalism. The Second Great Awakening, a great evangelical movement in the early 1800s, championed the abolition of slavery. By the late 19th century, evangelicalism had virtually merged with the liberal political movement for free silver, which aimed to give debtors relief from creditors by lowering the value of money.

Then in 1896, William Jennings Bryan, the Democratic candidate for president, and the leading evangelical politician in the country, conducted his campaign against big business by accusing it of trying to "crucify man on a cross of gold and pressing down on man's head a crown of golden thorns." Christian imagery drove the campaign that Bryan ran. His rhetoric was full of biblical links to politics. Bryan lost in 1896, lost again in 1900, and, yes, again in 1908, each time advocating more liberal ideas such as the right to vote for women, a progressive income tax, and government ownership of railroads. In 1916, he resigned as Secretary of State rather than deliver a note to Germany that he believed would bring America into World War I. Bryan was also a pacifist.

By 1925, however, science had become part of the mix of American political and religious life. Charles Darwin had explained life's beginnings scientifically by evolution in a way not found in the

Bible. And fundamental faith in the Bible was the rock on which the evangelical movement was built for 16 centuries. Before Darwin, religious faith had been fact and science theory. After Darwin, the roles were reversed. Thus Bryan and his evangelicals took up the cause against science and in favor of the Tennessee law, which Scopes, a schoolteacher, was charged with violating. Bryan was even named a prosecutor in the trial.

H.L. Mencken was the premier journalist of his day, also one of America's leading liberal writers. His whole philosophy was grounded on science as the basis for modern government. Mencken disdained the faith of evangelicals and wrote faith was, "an illogical belief in the occurrence of the improbable." He hated Bryan as a symbol of that faith. Mencken saw a chance to destroy Bryan and his evangelical faith at the Scopes trial. He persuaded his friend Clarence Darrow to work with the ACLU on the defense. The result was a circus, not a trial, in which Darrow humiliated Bryan with a brilliant cross-examination of Bryan as an expert on the Bible. When the "great commoner" died five days later, Darrow, the ultimate cynic, said, "A man who for years had fought excessive drinking, now lies dead from indigestion caused by overeating."

Mencken and his fellow journalists covering the Scopes trial turned Bryan's humiliation into a disaster for his evangelical religion. Science, and particularly science as an explanation of life, triumphed in America's press. Evangelicalism became a national joke synonymous with the "boobs" Mencken denounced in his newspaper column. Wounded, evangelicalism retreated out of the spotlight and out of politics.

Richard Nixon, however, sensed its power in America's midwest heartland and south where it was based. Gradually in the 1960s and 1970s, he coaxed evangelicalism back into political life, this time as an ally of the right, not the left. By 2004, 80,000 evangelical church members were ready to march against science on today's life issues of contraception, abortion, and stem cell research, with gay marriage added for good measure. That march made the difference for George Bush. Liberalism had missed a critical point when it tied itself to science. Evangelicals vote, science doesn't.

Last summer *The Morning Call* ran a story on its back pages. A group called "Americans Standing for God and Country" were starting a political tour trucking the Ten Commandments monument which had been barred by an ACLU lawsuit from an Alabama courthouse around the country. The idea was to mobilize support from evangelicals in the election. The tour was to conclude with a rally called "Americans for Jesus" in Washington. Its first stop was Dayton, Tennessee.

Two Mayors and a Lawyer

Building a Stadium
December, 2004

One of my last pieces on a local issue; I turned out to be wrong at least for now. The park and the Iron Pigs are a great success; but the cost to the taxpayers has been great as well.

On February 5, 1925, my grandfather, Allentown Mayor Malcolm W. Gross, urged the city's athletic groups to work together to build a large stadium. During the 1920s, Allentown saw a new public high school, the PPL tower, and the Americus Hotel, all successfully constructed. Those projects made economic sense and had community support, which resulted in their completion. But no stadium was built. My grandfather's trial balloon turned out to be filled with lead. There was no community support, so it didn't happen.

Things are a bit different here today as we watch the unfolding drama (or comedy) of efforts to build a 7,000 seat, minor league ballpark at a cost of $29 million dollars. Whether we will get such a stadium here is not yet clear. However, the process has made some other equally important things very clear.

First, this project, like my grandfather's big stadium of the 1920s, has no community support. The big new stadium will be built only if the money for it can be found somewhere other than Allentown. A big part of that problem was solved by a $12 million state grant. However, the condition of that grant requiring a "local" match only served to demonstrate that we don't want to pay for the new ballpark. Well-intentioned legislators tried to solve the "local" contingency by proposing a tax on out-of-town hotel guests, or that the state match its own money and call it "local". Nothing could better demonstrate the fact that our own town wasn't willing to pay for this deal.

Second, the process exposed fissures in the whole concept of Lehigh and Northampton Counties as one Lehigh Valley. In fact, the two counties fought each other for the state money. Northampton County's representatives wanted the grant to go to the half-complete monument to a previous failure of minor league baseball off Route 78 in Williams Township. More interesting perhaps, Allentown couldn't agree on a site within its own boundaries. City officials wanted a downtown location. But club owners affiliated with major league baseball used that affiliation as a trump card with the governor to require that the stadium be at the Agere location on the east side. The idea was that an affiliated team had a better chance of success. No one seemed to notice that the affiliated team would apparently be transferred from another town where it had already failed, or that the Allentown Ambassadors had folded this year after several seasons of failing to sell seats at a much smaller park. Where were the customers going to come from for the larger park? And there was the *The Morning Call's* recent analysis, which showed that minor league ball in other cities brought little or no economic benefit to the community. Yet the money coming from the state was supposed to be an economic development grant.

Why are we chasing this plan for a white elephant at this point? Bill White's *Morning Call* column the other day made the only remaining arguments for it. First, it will promote community spirit. A good point if the new stadium was near the Allentown community, or any community for that matter. It's not. It's on an industrial site near Route 22. So, we are going to take industrial land off the tax rolls to put up a ball field, which is nowhere near anything except a congested highway. Second, Bill argued, if we don't take the money some other city will. True enough in today's cynical political climate, but can you really build a community project in this community based on state handouts for something no one here thinks is a good idea?

Sunday, December 26th
January, 2005

Friends liked this piece on Bush and his lack of response to the Tsunami, and I got several compliments on it.

Sunday, December 26th — news reports all day of a great tidal wave in the Indian Ocean. Large numbers are dead and many more injured. We hear nothing from President Bush who is vacationing in Texas.

Monday, December 27th — newspaper front pages estimate 12,000 dead in half a dozen countries. The State Department says we will give $3 million dollars towards relief, but we still hear nothing from the president.

Tuesday, December 28th — the number of dead is now reported on the front pages to be 20,000 or more. The president doesn't read the papers. The Administration, however, swings into action and attacks a UN official for criticizing the west as "stingy." The government now commits $35 million for relief.

Wednesday, December 29th — the Administration wins a complete victory over the UN as the official involved "clarifies" his statement by saying he wasn't referring to this particular disaster. The Red Cross now estimates the number dead at over 100,000. NPR announces on its morning news that the president will be making a statement later in the day. The president makes the statement, but there is no change in the $35 million dollar commitment.

Thursday, December 30th — news organizations report that the "socialist government" of Spain is giving $68 million to the relief. Questions to the White House as to whether some of the $40 million dollars already raised for the president's inauguration might go to the relief are rebuffed with the answer that those are private funds. Couldn't the president have at least made a call to some of his friends who are paying $2,500 to have breakfast with him on inauguration day and request that their private funds be switched to help in the disaster?

Friday, December 31st - the president issues a statement that the US is now upping its contribution to $350 million. Secretary of State Powell says this is not a change of policy, only a response to the unfolding situation.

Saturday, January 1st — the number of dead is now estimated at over 150,000 with 5 million homeless. The president devotes his Saturday morning radio address to the disaster.

Regardless of whether the Administration changed policy when it upped our contribution to $350 million dollars, there was an important change in policy before the disaster in mid-December, which was not widely reported. The Bush Administration reduced its contribution to global aid programs aimed at helping poor nations. It told The Save the Children Fund and Catholic Relief Services that it wouldn't honor earlier funding promises. Apparently, the huge deficit which the government is running made it necessary for the Administration to concentrate what little money it had left for international humanitarian crises not preventive action. Tragically, this new crisis-only policy was quickly put to a terrible test by the tsunami.

It was an awful week for those living around the Indian Ocean rim, and a bad week for the United States as we tried to play catch up in recognizing that a catastrophe of biblical proportions had occurred. There are three possible explanations for what came close to another foreign policy fiasco with America acting against its own best interests and instincts.

First, President Bush could be a callous fool and his Administration cheapskates. That is unlikely based on hearing the president Wednesday. Mr. Bush was obviously genuinely upset about the loss of life, especially the children.

Second, the Administration could have been worried about being perceived by its right wing as favoring "foreign aid." Foreign aid has been a whipping boy of the Republican right wing for decades. It's equated to welfare here at home by those in the Republican Party who believe it is nothing more than a handout to a bunch of lazy corrupt foreigners. The president has done slightly better than past administrations regarding our international obligations to the poor by at least getting America's foreign aid up to $15 billion dollars per year. He also tried to promote The Millennium Fund which was to aid developing nations. That failed because of the usual opposition in the Republican House of Representatives. The failure was probably enough to give Mr. Bush pause before he leaped to the relief of people in faraway countries with strange sounding names.

Third, and linked to the second reason, was the fact that the United Nations was so prominently featured in relief efforts during the early days of the tragedy. The only thing the Republican right wing hates more than the concept of foreign aid is the United Nations. That may explain why the president wanted to be seen as putting together his own coalition to coordinate relief efforts.

Regardless, the Bush Administration is now on the issue—it has to be. We can't go on dealing with world poverty and illness only on a crisis basis, although we need to forcefully respond to what has just happened. Just as important, we can't go on, as the State Department's own website concedes, being the country with "the smallest among government foreign assistance programs." We can't go on giving .14% of the total of our national economy to the poor abroad and spending $450 billion on the defense department at the same time. We need to start prioritizing want over war.

Pope John Paul Shows Grace in His Notion of "Greatness"

February, 2005

I was pleased with this piece about an obscure failed Emperor of Austria/Hungary. It drew an angry letter to the Editor reminding me that I violated Canon law with my comments.

There is such a thing as a splendid failure – General George Armstrong Custer, for example. Emperor Charles Hapsburg was not one of those. Charles was just an outright flop as the last ruler of the ramshackle empire of Austria-Hungary. He and his empire finally collapsed in 1918. Losing an empire that had existed in various iterations since 1526 is not easy, but Charles did it.

Described as "shifty" by historian Robert Kann, Charles ruled only two years. His life ended in exile on April Fools' Day, 1922, after two pitiful failed attempts to return to power in the rump state of Austria – all that remained of the once vast Hapsburg lands in central Europe.

Why then, did Pope John Paul II recently beatify Charles, an honor only one step away from sainthood in the Catholic Church? Pope John Paul and his predecessors have seldom favored kings and emperors as saints. St. Louis, the King of France who led two crusades, is the only name that comes readily to mind in that category, but that was almost 1,000 years ago.

The Pope's choice in the case of Emperor Charles is apparently rooted in two things Charles did during his brief tenure as a ruler. First, when he beatified him, the Pope said that Charles attempted (badly, as he did with everything else) to start peace negotiations. He failed, of course, but he was virtually the only world leader to at least make an effort to do so. (Pope Benedict and President Woodrow Wilson were the others who even tried).

There was a second facet of Charles' brief career that I suspect brought him to John Paul's attention. Charles commuted the death sentence of an assassin who had murdered Austria-Hungary's prime minister, and he granted amnesty to a Czech patriot convicted of high treason who was also sentenced to death.

Charles' Austria-Hungary lost 1.3 million of its subjects in the war its inept emperor tried to stop. By that standard, the Iraq War is still a minor conflict, but it has now killed well over 100,000 Iraqis, according to a John Hopkins University survey completed last year. It has killed more than 1,400 Americans as well. Still it goes on.

President Bush, who started it, said recently that he favors "a culture of life." That statement is hard to reconcile with the deaths this war has caused for Iraqis and the Americans. It is also hard to reconcile the 150 executions of criminals that Mr. Bush presided over as governor of Texas.

Perhaps the explanation for the apparent selective application of Mr. Bush's "culture of life" philosophy is that he aspires to the greatness of history. He has described himself as the war president and seems to relish appearances before cheering troops in military get-ups, so he may see himself as a candidate for the title of "great."

History has awarded "great" to few people. Almost all of them won the laurel because of military excess. For example, Frederick the Great of Prussia started a series of European wars solely to enlarge the Prussian state. He embedded the concept of preventive war in German military theory, and left behind a powerful military state, bankrupt financially and morally, which shortly after collapsed, in yet another war. Mr. Bush has made preventive war the centerpiece of American foreign policy.

Pope John Paul had something quite different from this view of historical greatness in mind when he moved Emperor Charles so close to sainthood. Everyone knows Lord Acton's famous principle about the corrupting aspects of power. Few, however, know his rejoinder, "Which is why so few great men are good men."

Pope John Paul, although ailing now, values highly the goodness of men like Emperor Charles, and I would be willing to bet, disdains those who seek greatness of war.

George F. Kennan
April, 2005

George Kennan has always fascinated me, so his death ended something for me. I tend to identify with national figures past and present perhaps more than I should and give them qualities perhaps more than they have.

George F. Kennan died at the age of 101 last month. George Washington, who died in 1799, had something in common with Kennan besides a first name. Washington's Farewell Address, which was actually not a speech, but rather a sort of essay released to the Philadelphia press, warned against America becoming entangled with foreign alliances. Washington's warning became the first commandment of U.S. foreign policy for well over the next century.

Kennan's "Long Telegram" from Moscow, where he was serving in our Embassy in 1946, and his "X article" in the *Journal of Foreign Affairs* laid out the strategy of "containment" for America in the face of a powerful Soviet Union's worldwide ambitions. Despite a rocky road, containment became the basis of U.S. policy for the next four decades. As Assistant Secretary of State, Kennan later successfully implemented his idea with the Truman Doctrine which saved Greece from communism and the Marshall Plan which saved all of Western Europe. No state paper since the Farewell Address has had anything close to such an effect on our international relations.

I say rocky road because containment was intended, Kennan said, to cure, "Washington's of naïve optimism" about the Russians. Kennan believed that the Kremlin was "highly sensitive to the logic of force." However, he also believed that the Soviets did not want war, and that, at bottom, their system was rotten and sure to collapse of its own totalitarian weight given time. America needed, therefore, to ready itself for a political not a military struggle. Although containment was unpopular with both Democratic Secretary of State Dean Atchison, and his successor, Republican John Foster Dulles, as being too soft on communism, and although Stalin had Kennan declared persona non grata as too much of a hawk, containment remained American policy throughout the entire Cold War.

In the long run, Kennan proved right and showed us a middle way between war and appeasement. Containment provided a safe bridge from George Washington's isolationism to today's world dominance.

Surprisingly, Kennan did not regard the Long Telegram and "X" article as his most important writing on policy. Instead, he put a paper he wrote for the State Department in 1950 "The Atomic Bomb and the choices for American Policy" in that category. In it, Kennan argued strongly against the expansion of our nuclear program. Instead, he proposed international control of these weapons, putting limits on their numbers, and a possible complete elimination of them. Kennan's views were rejected by President Truman, and America developed the first hydrogen bomb. The Soviets quickly followed down the road America had paved, and so, now, have the British, French, Chinese, Israelis, Indians, Pakistanis, and probably North Koreans. Iran is apparently not far behind. Ironically, the weapon we invented to give us ultimate power is now the principal thing denying us that power. Possession of a handful of nuclear weapons will or already has made North Korea and Iran immune from the thousands of nuclear warheads we possess. Even more ironic, these weapons are useless to us in the struggle against terror. On the other hand, one of them in terrorists' hands could do us incalculable harm.

So far, no administration since the Berlin Wall came down in 1988 has had any answer to this gigantic failure of policy or the huge threat nuclear weapons pose. We have winked at our so-called friends in Pakistan who have sold information on the bomb like candy and blustered at enemies like North Korea, all to no effect. In truth, we have no meaningful policy regarding nuclear weapons, yet they are the greatest threat to us and all humanity.

Perhaps Kennan's idea that the problem is political not military gives us a clue towards a middle way, which will have a goal of getting rid of all these weapons including ours. If we engage every country that has these weapons, including ourselves, in meaningful discussions about how to eliminate them, we can move toward that goal. Up to now, we have stayed in the background, and hinted we might be willing to pay off Iran and North Korea if they give up their weapons programs or attack them if they don't. However, we have never conceded that all nuclear weapons are a world problem. Our nuclear weapons, together with those of our "friends," need to be on the negotiating table, as well as those of countries we perceive as threatening us, to make any real progress. And we need desperately to address the problem with a new approach when we enter those negotiations ourselves. This problem is too important to leave to our friends.

The Spirit of Key West, Florida
May, 2005

Key West is one of those places Janet and I fell in love with on two brief visits. It's so unlike the rest of America.

Nothing better captures the spirit of Key West, Florida than its airport. It is a small, out of date, 1960s sort of place where passengers are packed together on benches as they try to cope with omnipresent airline security. The airport has a single TV sitting high up, like every other American airport. However, as opposed to the ubiquitous CNN, which blares forth in every other terminal, Key West displays a TV evangelist on its screen. You can't hear the fellow's sermon. His message about salvation is trumped by the PA system, which blares out racy Spanish love songs. No one watches or listens to either one. That's the key to Key West.

The town itself is full of even more glaring contrasts, which are also blithely ignored by those who created them. It has, of course, a significant gay population. In fact, if you mention you are going to Key West, people will invariably wait a respectful sentence or two and then, attempting to be casual, mention that one is likely to see gays there. The remark is generally made much like the mention that there are palm trees in a place. And, in fair truth, one does see men walking arm in arm and women embracing and kissing in Key West. The same sort of thing we saw hour after repetitive hour on TV last year when the great debate was rocking America over gay marriage. In Key West, in person, it really doesn't seem like much of a much. Right up against this gay presence, and not being the least concerned with it, are good old boys from the deepest Deep South. You know the pickup truck, cowboy hat, and confederate flag types.

But that's not all of the contrasts. Spanish is spoken everywhere. The place is full of Latinos. It also has a large and longstanding black population. And there are plenty of homeless people visible around the town and on the beaches as well. No one is noticeably upset by any of these different types who, elsewhere in America, form the flash points for our cultural and values wars.

Meanwhile, there is a housing boom in town, too. However, again it is very different from the boom going on in the rest of the country which is why First Lady Laura Bush recently named Key West one of eight Preserve America Communities. They don't tear down any housing in Key West and build large oversize houses on undersized lots. Instead, they restore what's there. The result is a mix of housing architecture much like the town's mix of people and lifestyles. It's delightful to walk around (you can walk in Key West) and drink in all that difference somehow working in each neighborhood. When we tear houses down we do two things, both of which are bad.

First, we drive out the entire community living there, breaking it up and usually making it impossible to re-form somewhere else. Second, we destroy the subtle organization of a neighborhood's homes worked out over decades which provides access, privacy, and style.

It may be that Key West works so well with its crazy quilt of people and houses because of its great warm weather. It seems to rain only at night, and frost is as unknown as palm trees are to us. Good weather makes for good moods and tolerance. For much the same reason, people are on vacation there, which generates happy moods during which they forget their natural animosities. But somehow it works.

Yet, there is something more there, too; an attitude which starts in the town itself, works itself into its residents' psyches and envelopes its visitors. An attitude which proves, at least on this island, so distant it is barely part of the continental U.S., that we can all get along, and when we do, it makes for such a better life.

Office of the Chief Justice of the United States

May, 2005

The idea to reestablish consensus seemed like a worthwhile topic.

Only two offices in today's world have real power and life tenure — the Pope and chief justice of the United States. One hundred plus men in red have just chosen the first. With Chief Justice William H. Rehnquist ailing and eighty, the President will soon choose the second.

Given the importance which liberals and conservatives now attach to our federal courts generally, and to the chief justices in particular, the President's decision will surely be the political theater of 2005. George W. Bush made clear from the beginning of his first term that he would not repeat his father's mistake of neglecting his party's right wing. And he has surely not done so. From his first appointment of attorney general — the Bible thumping John Ashcroft to his recent choice of UN-bashing John Bolton for United Nations Ambassador, Bush has shown that when the right wing cared about a major appointment, he would serve up someone to their liking.

The chief justice's job is by far the biggest appointment (or so the interest groups lead us to believe) to come up for grabs. It controls legal philosophy throughout the entire court system, and because of the court's decision in *Marbury v. Madison,* over two hundred years ago, the chief justice leads a court which alone decides what the Constitution means.

Who will the President choose? Justice Antonin Scalia is the only name which stands out. True, there are other possibilities in the lower courts (Wilkinson, Alito, and Luttig), but Justice Scalia has the only star power with the right wing. Perhaps as important, he is a close friend of Dick Cheney.

Scalia, as a chief justice candidate, has other right wing advantages as well. The President always cites him as one of the two members of the Court he considers models for the bench. He is a devout Catholic who, in a recent speech in Louisiana, praised "traditional Catholics" who "follow religiously the teachings of the Pope." He is an avid hunter. He has one son who served in Iraq, another who is an official in the Bush Administration, and another who is a priest. And he was confirmed as a Justice unanimously by the Senate, making it difficult for Democrats to now oppose him for another position on the same court.

His age, 69, is against him — Bush likes young judges who will influence the courts for as many decades as possible. But the Cardinals just elected a 78 year old, so Scalia is a mere pup by that standard.

Most importantly, Scalia has a constitutional philosophy which seems to dovetail with the right wing's bitter hatred of activist judges. He believes in using "original meaning" to interpret the Constitution. Original meaning was actually first proposed by Judge Bork, who became a folk hero for the right wing after the Senate shot down his nomination to the Court.

It is a theory which says you look only to what people understood a constitutional provision to mean at that time when it was written when you enforce it today. What was actually intended by the drafter is irrelevant, as is all history since that time. For example, originalists claim the 8th Amendment forbidding "Cruel and unusual punishments" does not mean the death penalty is cruel and unusual because every major crime carried a death sentence when the 8th Amendment was enacted in 1791. By the same originalists' logic, segregation should not have been barred by the Equal Protection provision in the 14th Amendment because segregated schools were the norm in 1868 when the Amendment was passed.

Justice Scalia does not say the death penalty cannot be abolished or that segregation is a good thing, but as a believer in absolute democracy, he holds that only the Legislature, not the Supreme Court interpreting the Constitution, can make those kinds of changes. Thus, unless a minority right was spelled out and understood to be a right when it became part of the Constitution, it does not have any life before the Supreme Court. That leaves a Supreme Court interpreting the Constitution with little to do. As Dawn Johnsen, Professor of Constitutional Law at Indiana University said recently in the *Christian Science Monitor*, "Initially, originalism is very appealing because it promises an easy answer to every question, but it is a lie. It has the effect of freezing constitutional meaning at a time when only white, propertied men were fully protected under the law."

Except for Justice Clarence Thomas, who seems to agree with him, Scalia has had no success in convincing any of his colleagues to adopt his theory, which would essentially leave the protection of most minority rights in the hands of the majority in Congress. Cynics say that is because it would also take away much of the power his fellow justices have accumulated over the two hundred years of the Republic by virtue of their own decisions. Idealists say it would virtually end the idea that the Courts can protect minority rights. Without a Supreme Court acting to protect obvious injustices in the society, its victims would be left in the hands of an often callous and more often simply inactive Congress

This might be just as well for those who would deprive the Courts of any real role in the constitutional process. However, the last time that happened we ended up in a civil war because the legislative and executive branches were unable to resolve the slavery crises. Regardless, before he acts, Mr. Bush also needs to consider the other prong of original meaning. The President's power is limited in the same way. In fact, Scalia wrote a biting dissent (nothing unusual there) in 2004 criticizing Bush's claim that the President had implied power to hold US citizens indefinitely by charging them as enemy combatants. The Constitution reserved questions of liberty to the courts, not the President, Scalia said. In other words, Scalia may not like activist judges, but he doesn't seem to like activist presidents either.

Two Mayors and a Lawyer

Reading the Declaration of Independence on July 4th
July, 2005

The Morning Call ran this as a major piece. I think it plays well even a few years later.

In the small villages of New England they do something odd on Independence Day — they read the entire Declaration of Independence. No one reads public papers out loud anymore. Newspapers print them, or they sit under glass in dusty museums. No one actually hears what's in them the way Americans did when they were first issued. The Declaration was first presented as a public reading (perhaps shouting), to the American people, and it is meant to be heard. However, that takes a little time, a little effort, a little listening, and a good deal of thought after you listen. We don't have the time or energy to do that today. TV saturated brains can't take the 10 or 20 minutes of sustained listening necessary to appreciate something like the Declaration of Independence. That's why it's such a strange experience to walk down Main Street with your dog or child behind a rag-tag local drum and bugle corps, and then form up in no particular order on a little grass square and hear the Declaration as people did in 1776.

As you listen, you hear first the familiar and famous words "truths, self-evident," "all men created equal," "endowed by their creator with certain unalienable Rights," "Life, Liberty, and the Pursuit of Happiness." Then comes the rest of the words, words that indict George III King of England. George of Hanover, bewigged, portly, and often insane during his long reign, is bitterly attacked in line after line, and then charged with all forms of tyranny against his American subjects — refusing to assent to laws, undercutting local legislatures, interfering with Judges' tenure and cutting off their salaries, making the military power supreme over the civil power, taxing without consent, and denying trial by jury, to name only a few of his many crimes. Why are so many words of this foundation of our country a litany of wrongs by a hapless king? There are two reasons: one looking back and the other forward.

For the intense six years preceding the Declaration and intermittently previous to that, the colonists carefully maintained a fiction. They claimed to be loyal subjects to the King while quarreling with his Parliament. Their disputes, they said, were about taxes and policies enacted by a series of parliaments and their prime ministers, not anything the King was doing. They had no beef with His Majesty. In this way, they avoided being branded as traitors and attempted to bridge the divided loyalties between American loyalists, like William Allen, and themselves. The fiction was finally exposed as a fig leaf when King George rejected a final offer of compromise in 1775. George proclaimed the Continental Congress and all Americans guilty of "rebellion and sedition," and his troops invaded Boston. At that point, there was nothing to do but face the truth. America's differences were with the King himself. However, in order to face that truth, Thomas Jefferson had to explain why the sudden shift to the King as the cause of all our troubles.

That's why the indictment of George III in the Declaration is so brilliant. Politically, Jefferson did not, as he said, aim "at originality of principle or sentiments," rather he adopted the arguments which his hearers already knew. Thus, he put them in a new format, which even today makes the colonists' case so effective. In politics it is always better to state the obvious, but in an unconventional way. Jefferson did.

However, a second problem also confronted Jefferson because the Declaration of Independence, while solving the question of loyalty by dissolving sovereignty, left open the question of what would happen to the new government if some of its subjects decided on a similar Declaration in the future. Jefferson doesn't really answer that question, and revolutionary that he was, he may not have wished to. Instead he counseled only "prudence" before any government is changed for "light or transient causes."

Jefferson also gave no explanation of how the new government would define and implement his strong words about equality, unalienable rights, and liberty. What did they mean as a basis for the new government?

Indeed, the questions of sovereignty and what liberty and equality meant, which the Declaration raised but did not answer were essentially evaded in America for the next ninety-one years until the terrible blood bath of the Civil War answered them by force. The Federal Government was thereafter clearly indissoluble. It alone would decide their meaning.

That, in itself, is a wonderful, but also terrifying thing. Wonderful because our achievements, economic and democratic, here and abroad, could never have been reached without an unbreakable center of our power. However terrifying, as well, because that center of power is now impregnable. It is now subject not to dissolution, but only to check by our other institutions. Those institutions, our democratic election process, our courts, press, and states, are vital to preserving our freedom and must not be corrupted by federal power. Thus, it is all the more important that when we celebrate the Declaration, we also recognize how important those institutions and those checks are to our freedom as well.

This wedding photo of my father and mother outside The Cathedral Church of St. Catharine of Siena after their marriage in 1934. Since it was a "mixed" marriage (he was Lutheran) they had to be married in the rectory, not in the church. My mother never forgot that slight.

The Coffee Craze
September, 2005

I have now become addicted to espresso and coffee shops. Even at Starbucks, I sit there and pretend I am a Frenchman sitting on the Boulevard.

White letters on the blackboard offer mint mocha chip cappuccino, caramel café macchiato, toffee nut latte and assorted iced coffees with cream. This is a coffee shop or perhaps a "coffee house," and like Chinese Restaurants, you can now find them anywhere in the U.S. offering almost exactly the same type of fare.

These coffee places are actually the second reincarnation of the English coffee houses, which arrived in London circa 1680. Turkish armies were then pushing into the center of Europe and bringing their coffee beans with them. The result was a great defeat for the Turks at Vienna, but a complete conquest of the Europeans and particularly the British taste buds by coffee. The coffee house serving the new drink became a sensation in London.

There was a political side to the coffee craze as well. People could talk and make political plans as they sipped their coffee. Those who opposed the Royal Government now had a place to meet and plot political strategies outside the king's court, which was controlled by the Tories. The result was the creation of the Whig party, possibly the first opposition political party in the world. The King and the Tories were so worried they considered closing down the coffee houses, but found they couldn't without creating a huge hole in the Royal budget due to lost taxes on coffee. So, the coffee house stayed, and Whigs went on to take over the government and elect Britain's first Prime Minister, Robert Walpole, in 1721.

The coffee house rose again in America in the 1960s. It was then the focal point of the anti-Vietnam War movement and the radical left. People went there to strum guitars, sing protest songs, hear poetry, and sometimes smoke dope. When a coffee house was proposed for Allentown in 1963, my father, Mayor Jack Gross, invoked zoning laws to stop it, and *The Morning Call* sarcastically referred to its "bearded" owner. *The Morning Call* missed the irony that the year before everyone in town had grown a beard for the city's Bicentennial.

Today's coffee house is slick and modern and a wonderful example of how American democracy and capitalism work to dominate us. People talk constantly, often on cell phones, but say nothing.

Note two things about the white lettered items on that board. First, coffee is way down on the list. Instead, syrupy sweet drinks dominate, designed to permit drinkers to claim they drink coffee, but not have to taste that black bitter stuff. That's the way American democracy works. Everyone can get in on the action, even if they don't like what the action is all about. The martini is another example of our democracy at work. In my dad's day it was a drink for the in-group, and the only decision was dry or very dry — meaning practically straight gin. Today, you can get chocolate martinis. James Bond would have been horrified.

Chocolate martinis and coffee houses with iced lattes do tell us something more about the way our country works. In other countries, the elite starts a fad, and the masses copy it as closely as possible. When tea hit Britain, the lower classes aped their noble betters and drank it straight. They would never have thought of putting chocolate in it. Here, Americans seize on the pleasures of the rich, and then change them beyond recognition into something they like. But they keep the brand name so they have it both ways.

Then there is American capitalism at work. Look at the prices of those lattes. A bit more than a humble cup of java the Whigs drank in London and a lot more than espresso buried at the bottom of the sign.

My Friend Tom and I Share Fall Birthdays
October, 2005

I was getting old and it was time to apply for Social Security.

My longtime friend Tom Christman and I share fall birthdays, making it natural that we celebrated our 21st birthday touring Allentown's taprooms demanding to be carded. That major milestone, having passed in our lives, it seemed only fitting that we should attempt to repeat the process for our 65th birthday, but in a fashion more conducive to our graying hair. Thus, we applied together for Medicare.

We arrived at the Allentown office of Social Security shortly after 1:00 pm and found a neat modern facility with about 30 seats, all of which were quickly filling up with people who had one thing in common. They were a great deal younger than we were.

As we do now at every government or public facility in America, we went through security. Here we encountered the first of a series of government employees who were uniformly pleasant, helpful, and, most of all, patient.

As usual, there was a long line at security, conversations going on and on with the officer in charge and with little progress. However, eventually we got to the head of the line, were given a number, and told to return to our seats. At this point, I became aware of the large color photos on the wall. Mr. Bush was on the left. There's a bit of irony there. On the right was a woman who apparently had no name, or at least none she wanted me to know. In the middle was the vice president with the right side of his mouth pointing upward in the sneer that has come to be recognized as his version of a tight-lipped smile. That drew my attention to his eyes staring straight at me. Were those eyes moving? Here was real security.

I was 90. My number was called. I reported to window 3 where I was informed that I had to come back for an "appointment" because I was not in the "system." I thought I had been in the "system" since 1958 when the government started taking money from my paycheck for social security. Apparently that was a different "system." A day later, I returned for my appointment and was confronted by security again. Social Security and security are two different things in America. Social Security makes you feel secure. Security doesn't. I am not sure either do much else. In any event, this time I was given a receipt stating, "you have successfully checked in for your appointment." What a relief. To make things even better, my receipt informed me that I would be called by name. I had progressed from being just a number.

My "appointment" took about an hour. My dog-eared original Social Security card was almost a problem because no one has them anymore. Also, I didn't have my birth certificate. Who carries that around? Fortunately, I was permitted to mail my birth certificate to my interviewer. Otherwise, I would have had to return for yet another "appointment" to deliver it personally to him.

If all goes well, I may be part of the "system" in a few more months when I get my official Medicare card. Of course, I still don't know if I should have signed up for Medicare Plan B, which was explained to me, but it seems unexplainable even by the patient people at Social Security. Tom, who is a CPA, can't figure it out either. If I understand it right, no matter what I do, I will pay more money to the government for a benefit I may or may not need. I thought after age 65 you got money from the government.

I will have to repeat some or all of this process in six months when I apply for Social Security. You would think it all could be done in one fell swoop, but social security is yet another different "system." However, since I will then be a part of the Medicare "system," I will have an edge and may be not required to spend two days being watched by the vice president to make sure I am who I am. So, what is to be learned from my daunting experience?

First, America's overwhelming concerns today are security and fraud. Everyone in the government from the grim grinning Mr. Cheney down is trying to protect us from those twin evils. Second, once you are in a "system," you are carried along with no responsibility for yourself and no control over what that particular "system" does or does not do for you.

Next, the battle to end welfare in our time has been won by dumping people out of the "welfare system" and into the "Social Security system." Those twenty- and thirty- somethings waiting in the social security office are very likely there to apply for Social Security disability payments. This is yet another "system." Whether this change of "system" accomplished anything in their lives is another question.

Next, I have lines, appointments, and systems to look forward to in my golden years. Surely there should be something more. Finally, I wonder about a government obsessed with fraud and terror, rather than a government making our "systems" work.

Why Write about a White Woman on MLK Day?
January, 2006

An effort to honor Martin Luther King, Jr. Day by writing about Eleanor Roosevelt seemed to play well. Again, I got compliments, at least from friends.

Why write about a dead white woman on Martin Luther King Day? Why write about Eleanor Roosevelt at all? Eleanor is probably the best remembered and most detested name from the FDR years. The right-wingers have never forgiven her liberalism.

Yet, there is probably no other white person who did more, and certainly none who took more risk, political, and physical, to promote the rights of the "negro race" in the 1930s, 1940s, and 1950s. After Martin Luther King burst on the scene in the 1960's until her death November 7, 1962, no one, white or black, was more out front in her support of the complete and immediate end of segregation.

Eleanor's opposition to segregation was public and dramatic throughout FDR's first term, but it was during the second term that she really attracted the lightening of the racists who had dominated all phases of American life and law since the 1870s. In November 1938, at a public meeting in Birmingham, Alabama, she defied local segregation ordinances by pointedly moving her chair out of the white section of the audience to the middle of the aisle separating her from the Negros-only portion of the audience.

In 1939, Eleanor followed up by taking on the Daughters of the American Revolution, which had denied Marian Anderson, the noted black opera singer, the use of its Constitution Hall in Washington. Eleanor put her thumb in the eye of the DAR, the most powerful social and patriotic group in the U.S. First, she publicly resigned. Then she organized an open air concert for Anderson at the Lincoln Memorial.

In 1942, Eleanor pleaded with FDR to commute black sharecropper Odell Waller's death sentence by a Virginia jury from which blacks had been deliberately excluded. She even insisted on interrupting a war planning meeting of FDR's to try and save Waller from the electric chair. She failed, and the attention she had attracted by her unpopular efforts earned her more hatred.

After FDR's death in 1945, she fought on for civil rights for blacks. For her efforts, the Ku Klux Klan offered a $25,000 reward for anyone who would kidnap her. J. Edgar Hoover's FBI kept tabs on her instead of protecting her. There are 4,000 reports of spying on her by the Bureau in its files. Hoover, himself, believed she had colored blood. Eleanor carried her own pistol to protect herself, but she continued her stand against segregation and joined the board of the NAACP, and eventually presented Martin Luther King with a medal for his services to the cause.

However, Eleanor had identified a hidden flaw in the fight against segregation. Almost the entire legal struggle was against segregated schools. Yet Eleanor correctly saw that even if integration of schools happened it would be meaningless if segregated housing continued in America. Her efforts to mandate that new federal housing being built during and after World War II be integrated were unsuccessful during her lifetime. Ten days after her death, President Kennedy did bar segregation from federally financed housing. It was too late. By then, the suburbs beckoned, and whites fled their cities leaving behind the now de facto segregated city schools to poor blacks unable to afford to follow them.

Still Eleanor had done more than any other white person in the dark days before Martin Luther King to wake up America to the evil within itself. After her death, King paid her a tribute which well describes her efforts — "The impact of her personality and its unwavering dedication to high principle and purpose cannot be contained in a single day or era."

There Are Limits on Free Speech
May, 2006

I closed out my opinion writer career with a piece on my favorite topic of the First Amendment. For some time I had been getting as many rejections from The Morning Call as publications. I had run out of ideas as well. This piece shut down the game.

There are limits on free speech despite the First Amendment. Oliver Wendell Holmes famously wrote as one example, "you can't shout fire in a crowded theater." However, it surprises most people to learn that the First Amendment does not apply at all when the government speaks. When Uncle Sam is talking there are no limits on what he can or can't say. That's a significant, but unnoticed addition to other government powers.

That's why the government can put a poster saying, "Your Country Wants You," to get young people to join the army, even if some of its taxpayers, who pay for the posters, think war is a bad idea. That's why the government can honor all kinds of causes on its postage stamps, even if some of those pasting on the stamps don't like the cause honored.

In other words, government speech is pretty much at the discretion of those running the government at any given time. Pretty much, but not completely. Two recent federal cases coming out of the South demonstrate that no legal principle is ever bulletproof, and that the abortion debate is still raging and now touching even some arcane areas of jurisprudence.

The federal cases involve, of all things, license plates. More precisely, pro-life groups successfully lobbied South Carolina and then Tennessee to issue specialty license plates with the slogan, "Choose Life" on them. The money from the sale of plates then went back to pro-life causes or groups. Pro-choice groups were not given a right to have their own plates. No one who lives in America will be surprised to learn that court fights immediately erupted in both states. Pro-choice groups claimed that their constitutional rights have been violated. As Alexis de Tocqueville noted over 150 years ago, any political fight in America sooner or later ends up in court. And in court, things get complicated, as anyone who has been there will attest. First, a federal appeals court in South Carolina said that the state's license plate was unconstitutional.

However, the three judges hearing the case gave different reasons why. Then a federal appeals court in Tennessee heard much the same arguments about virtually the same Tennessee law. Two of those judges said Tennessee's law was fine under the constitution. A third, though, said it was not.

The reason for this confusion is not the inability or refusal of judges to read the law in front of them as is so often claimed. Rather, it is the collision of important and complex constitutional principles. On one hand is the idea that the government can say what it wants on army posters or stamps. On the other hand, however, is something called a public forum to which the First Amendment does apply. A public forum is the idea that once the government allows one side access to its property, it must allow opposing groups the same type of time and space.

The question that South Carolina and Tennessee have raised by their laws is whether license plates are government speech, or whether pro-life groups who are buying them and using them are getting access to government property by a special law. If the latter, then the state has created a public forum, and pro-choice groups must be allowed to speak in it as well. And the facts are mixed. The state issues the plate, but the pro-life group pays for it and uses it. Put another way, can the state rent to outside groups its broad power to speak as it wishes.

That's why different judges came to opposite results, and why the Supreme Court is being asked to resolve the question. It is fairly likely the Supreme Court will take a look at this case because otherwise federal law would be contradictory in two states and also because Chief Justice Roberts is the proponent of government speech.

If the Supreme Court does act and does decide the case, it will give one side or the other a victory, of sorts, in the never-ending battle over abortion. Such a victory will probably have little effect on the abortion fight itself, which seems literally and figuratively to have a life of its own. But no matter how they rule, justices can hardly be unaware of the potential political consequences in such a political case. Ironically, the result will have a much greater impact on free speech rights or the expansion of government power than on abortion. That is a consequence of so many political decisions, like abortion, being forced into our courts by the inability of our democracy to resolve them otherwise. As Holmes also said, "Great cases, like hard cases, make bad law."

My mother Agnes died February 2, 2007. I worked hard on these remarks at her memorial at St. Catharine's Cathedral. I think I did pretty well in capturing at least a small piece of the puzzle about my mother. She lived 100 years, dominated a good part of my life, and yet, I don't know that I ever really knew her. The Gross family and their family name tended to obscure her importance in making me what I am.

Thank you for all your support and kindness during this time of sadness for our family. I can't tell you how much your thoughtful calls and notes have meant to us. They really brought home how significant Agnes Gross was to all of us.

As I sat here today, I was struck that, before this church was here, my mother was here. Before the old church next door was here, my mother was here. Before this parish was here, my mother was here. In fact, when this parish was founded, Father Phelan ate dinner with her family every week because there was no rectory. She saw so many changes here over all those years, yet she would have been particularly pleased today to see these four young women as altar servers at her Memorial Mass.

There is a short story by the writer O. Henry, titled, "The Last Leaf," that I thought of often as I sat in this church on Sundays for the past year or so, first with my mother beside me and then, as she gradually failed, as I had to attend mass without her. The title seemed to exemplify my mother as she approached and then passed her 100th birthday last September 12th.

The story is about a man who has lost his will to live and stares constantly out his sickroom window at a vine from which one leaf after another blows away as winter arrives. Finally, a last leaf remains, and the man tells his friends that when it is gone, he will go too.

But the leaf clings stubbornly to the vine. Spring comes, and the leaf is still there. The man takes heart from the last leaf and recovers. Then comes one of those famous O. Henry trick endings. The last leaf is revealed to be a fake. It was painted on the vine by a friend to fool the sick man. It was only after my mother passed away, that I realized that the story was not only fiction, but false.

Agnes Lieberman Gross (she always used the L. even when she was first lady of Allentown, when my Dad was mayor) was, however, very like a last leaf, not just of her generation, but of a whole world now gone. A world without cars, planes, telephones, CDs, X-Boxes, nuclear bombs, and especially cell phones. A world of quiet, green space and peace on earth. That world had to give way to our world – had to let us make our world for good, bad or both. And even a last leaf as good and loved as my Mother had also to give way to the next generation and the next after that and the next after that. But, God gave her a chance to experience each of those generations - her grandchildren and even her great grandchildren - and they experienced her. What a wonderful life-changing experience it was for us. My mother was a many faceted woman, and we saw all of those facets in the long time we had with her. Today, I would like to mention just three which most impressed me.

First, there was her sense of family. In her case, it was the Lieberman family, a large rollicking Allentown German family starting with my grandparents "Doc and Ma," which expanded to eight grown children (three of whom still survive), 24 of my cousins, and lord only knows how many second cousins, cousins once removed, and third cousins. The Lieberman family was open to everyone. In addition to all those blood relatives, there were the numberless in-laws, stepchildren and even pets like our dog, Rusty. They were all Liebermans.

Second, was my Mother's sense of friendship. She was such a good friend to so many people. She showed us how being a good friend means giving of yourself and your time to others, not simply sucking dry the relationship by demanding others meet your needs. Her selflessness permitted those friendships to go on as long as she lived.

Third, my Mother had a sense of obligation to community. She always said, "There are too many chiefs and not enough Indians." I don't believe she ever chaired a single committee, was president of a single charity, or received a single medal or award. When we went through her things last week, there was her Red Cross volunteer pin, and a certificate from Meals on Wheels for her many years as a driver. When I went to grade school here she worked handing out lunches to us. She repeatedly gave of herself to Allentown and its needs. You would have a hard time looking over volunteer lists without finding her name. And she always took the thankless tasks. Even when she moved to Luther Crest she volunteered to serve on - the food committee (not exactly a glory job).

There are no trick endings in life and death, but there are memories of the leaves and lives that have gone before us. Agnes L. Gross gave us all wonderful memories and showed us how to live a modest, but meaningful life centered on our families and community. From that we can build much to hope for as we now move on without her. In one of my very last talks with her in the hospital, she said she had to get out soon so we could get a hot dog and a beer. We never got out to do that, but today we hope you will join us for some bratwurst and some beer at the Barrister's Club when this service concludes. My mother loved her beer (she was raised on it), so please join us and share some memories of her.

My Year with the Supreme Court
May, 2001

The Pennsylvania Supreme Court predates the Revolution. As far as I know, no one from Lehigh County had ever served as a law clerk to one of its justices. I was more than fortunate when Justice Michael J. Eagen offered me a clerkship. This is an account of my year working with him and its influence on my life.

My father died in 1964. I was then starting my final year at Villanova Law School. I hated law school and would return to my parents' home in Allentown as often as possible trying to convince my parents and myself that I should quit. Somehow my father coaxed me to go back each time with various plans of what I could do with my LLB (they didn't give JDs in those days) which would be more to my taste than a legal career. My father wasn't a lawyer, but he somehow had heard about clerkships, and said he would get me an Appellate Court clerkship when I finished law school. That kept me going until the start of my senior year when I was phoned from home and advised that he died suddenly of a heart attack.

I sleep walked through my final year of Villanova numbed by my father's death, and finally decided that I should at least apply for a clerkship as kind of a gesture to his memory. To my surprise, Supreme Court Justice Michael J. Eagen hired me at the then astounding salary of $7,500 per year. That was significantly more than any of my classmates, except the top man in the class who got $10,000 for a Third, Circuit clerkship.

In the 1960's only the Supreme and Superior Court judges in Pennsylvania had law clerks. The County Court judges had none. There was no Commonwealth Court.

In September 1965 when I started work, the Court consisted of Justice Eagen, Chief Justice John C. Bell, Jr., and the other associate Justices Musmanno, Cohen, Roberts, Jones, and O'Brien. The Chief Justice had two clerks and the rest one. Like today, the Court rode circuit sitting about six weeks in Philadelphia, four in Pittsburgh, and one in Harrisburg. We traveled with our justice. We got between $20 and $30 per day "expenses" plus "mileage" from our justice's hometown to where the Court was sitting. With the judicial rate of

$6 per day at the old Belleview Stratford Philadelphia and a $2 dinner at Horn and Hardart across the street, it was possible to save real money on our expense account. We lived in the hometown of our justice which for Eagen meant Scranton. In between sessions, I worked in the justice's private library in the Lackawanna County Courthouse. Every day I hand wrote memos on legal pads for Eagen based on my research.

Justice Eagen was a large man who somehow carried his significant girth with great ease. He had a huge face that was rather like one of those candle figures after they are partially melted. He seldom spoke; when he did, it was very quietly out of the side of his mouth. As a result, he commanded almost complete attention for every word he said. Eagen loved and was fascinated by the law. His opinions are still cited today in areas like defamation, real estate taxes, and felony murder. More important to those of us needing guidance in particular areas of law, they are invaluable as a Horn Book. They first give us the law, and then decide the case based on it.

Eagen was extremely adept at stitching together four justices to get the result he favored, and when he couldn't he wrote pointed brief dissents. He always read all of the briefs for every case the night before oral argument. I recall taking large stacks of paper books to his hotel room where he would prop himself up in bed and read and read the next day's cases. Yet, he seldom spoke from the bench. Only later, did I realize that he was informing himself for the justice's conference the morning after arguments where preliminary decisions were made as to how the court would rule on the previous days' cases. He wanted to be informed to win the votes he needed for a majority at that crucial conference.

Eagen had been forced to leave Harvard Law School by his own father's death and read law in Scranton after which he passed the bar. He became one of Lackawanna County's youngest District Attorneys, and the first Democrat elected to a countywide office. I have never known a more modest or charming man. When he became chief justice, several years after my clerkship, he guided the change in the Supreme Court to a certiorari court and presided over the new Appellate Court system. As usual, he did so quietly, but with tremendous effect.

Justices wrote their own opinions in 1965. Eagen, for instance, worked from his home in Scranton. Every night I would drop off my work. The next morning I would stop again and pick up the justice's handwritten opinions. Eagen could not sleep at night, so he worked nights on his opinions, which I then gave minor corrections, filled in the citations, and put in final form. We then put them on mimeographed blue copies and circulated them to the other justices for approval at the next session of the court.

The Court which I joined as a clerk had a national reputation. Chief Justice Bell was a forbidding figure with white hair, blue pinstripe suits and the craggy countenance of a Philadelphia lawyer. He was a former lieutenant governor who had served briefly as governor before going on the court. The other justices who were more or less on a first name basis with each other were permitted to call him "Chief." Everyone else addressed him as chief justice at all times. There were no time limits on Supreme Court arguments, but when the chief justice raised his pencil the wise advocate stopped and sat down immediately. The unwise heard the pencil tapped hard on the bench. That was as far as he ever had to go to cut off argument. Once when were in Harrisburg, Lieutenant Governor Ray Shaffer bounded down the Capitol steps as I was carrying Eagen's brief cases and walking the respectful five paces behind him and the chief justice. Shaffer clapped Bell on the back and boomed out, "Hi Jack." Bell did not even reply, he simply glared and walked on leaving his would be friend standing there.

Bell was regarded as the great defender of stare decisis and high conservatism in law particularly in the area of negligence. His opinions were strings of quotes from his earlier opinions with rather jarring unsupported conclusions, which always resulted in a plaintiff's case being dismissed. No new trials for him. Instead, common law doctrines, particularly contributory negligence, were ruthlessly applied to plaintiff's evidence even at the Appellate level ending their claims. For some reason he also hated the concept of a declaratory judgment and found any excuse to reject attempts to enforce the then relatively new Declaratory Judgment Act.

Justice Michael Musmanno was tall, slim and probably in his 70s in 1965. He never said a word to me in my entire year in the Court. He and Eagen had not spoken since the previous year when Eagen had cast the deciding vote against Musmanno in his failed challenge to obtain the Democratic senate nomination. Musmanno had some other personal dispute with Justice Herbert Cohen, and they also were not on speaking terms. Author of 15 books with a distinguished military career, Musmanno saw himself as the champion of the underdog. His great cause was a liberal interpretation of the common law of tort. This brought him into conflict with the chief justice on the meaning of the hoary common law doctrines of comparative negligence, charitable immunity, and so forth. Musmano dissents are florid literary works, and his views seldom commanded a majority, yet they got him national attention and the Court as well. Unnoticed, Musmanno was actually quite conservative in all other areas of the law, and paradoxically, almost automatically supported Bell's position outside of their disputes about the standards of negligence.

Justice Cohen, the court's third Democrat, had a mind like a razor. He applied his logic brutally in every case, and he could cut counsel to pieces during oral argument if their remarks were illogical. His opinions demonstrate the belief that logic is the supreme tool a court has to interpret the law. Justice Samuel Roberts, on the other hand, took a broader, more philosophical view of the law. He was willing to stretch a logical point to get to the result he wanted, but he did so with such broad verbal strokes that it is often difficult to see how he got there.

Justice Benjamin Jones was Eagen's best friend on the court. A small man with great energy, a progressive Republican, and a fellow coal cracker from Scranton's great rival city of Wilkes-Barre, Jones constantly surprised his colleagues especially in major cases, by siding with Eagen.

Justice Henry O'Brien today would be called a compassionate conservative. Quiet, perfectly groomed and dressed, he practically never spoke on the bench. He was a perfect gentleman. The chief justice could count on his vote.

Two other court officials require a comment, Patrick Bollsinger and William Fells. Bollsinger was prothonotary. As a favor, he completed my Supreme Court certificate of admission to the Bar in script. Bollsinger had been with the court a long time, perhaps back to the year when prothonotaries were required to write in script. In any event, he wielded significant power and seemed perpetually sad. Fells was the court crier and a former police officer. He was the closest thing I have ever seen to an English butler, always at the right hand of the justices and always ready to meet any of their needs.

The law was still a private men's club in 1965. Only one woman, Ann Alpern, had served briefly on the Supreme Court, and she had been defeated when she stood for election. I did see one African American, William Coleman, argue before the Court. Coleman was later secretary of transportation, and his brilliant presentation is literally the only one I remember out of the hundreds I heard during my year. Otherwise, it was a white man's world on both sides of the bench.

My year on the Supreme Court gave me a view of the law which would not have been possible from Allentown. I was the first law clerk from my hometown, and when I told my preceptor (we needed a preceptor and six months of work in a law office usually without pay to take the Bar in those days) of my good fortune, his only comment was that he didn't see any value in a year with the Supreme Court. He wanted me back in Allentown. Fortunately, I ignored his advice. Within a few months of my starting, the City of Philadelphia seized a Russian cargo ship claiming the Soviet Union owed it city taxes. I now realize that this was only one of the constant string of Cold War incidents. However, at the time, seeing important looking diplomats from Washington in a courtroom made me believe the court held the fate of the world in its hands. I should have noticed that both sides had hired big name law firms, a sure sign cooler heads would prevail and compromise the matter. They did.

Shortly after that, the Supreme Court, for the first and last time, drew the lines for the Assembly and Senate seats. Earl Warren's Supreme Court mandated one-man one vote under the Federal Constitution. Many similar mandates lay ahead especially in the criminal law where the Constitution quickly supplanted the common law and statutes, which our Supreme Court labored so hard to interpret for all of its previous history.

Although we didn't recognize it at the time, the great struggle over the common law of negligence between Bell and Musmano was also near its end. Eagen, Cohen, Jones, and Roberts were quietly moving away from the harsh results of the Chief Justice's view of negligence. Case by case, plaintiffs gained ground. The idea that jurors should decide cases became more appealing every day. More important, the principle that the common law could be abrogated completely by an act of the legislature was about to come into play. Within a few years, no fault, comparative negligence, and medical malpractice reform had undermined completely most of the court's common law decisions.

Perhaps most interesting was what we did not see. The great controversies of the 1960s, college riots, draft card burning, and the Vietnam War played themselves out in the federal courts, perhaps another sign that the Pennsylvania Supreme Court's jurisdiction and authority were giving way.

The Supreme Court's reapportionment of the House and Senate has long since been changed beyond the point of recognition. The Russians didn't start World War III over their freighter. The hundreds of cases the Supreme Court decided in my year in the Supreme Court (except for a few of Eagen's) are almost all nothing, but history. Yet, they all moved the law in a particular direction sometimes by tiny steps, sometimes by long jumps. That is the real significance of a high court decision. My year on the Supreme Court gave me a chance to watch that happen.

My First Client—Kathleen Hallman
May, 2001

Probably a new lawyer's most exciting, but also most frightening experience is his first case, especially a criminal case (where the stakes are high), and when he has never been in a courtroom, let alone handled a criminal trial before. This is my account of how Kathy Hallman's case and life story unfolded.

Kathy Hallman was my first client. Well, not my first paying client. She was a defendant in *Commonwealth v. Hallman* September Term of Lehigh County Court in 1966. I was her lawyer because of what the Supreme Court of the United States had done in *Gideon v. Wainwright* (1963). It had determined that the right to counsel in the 6th Amendment covered poor people (i.e. almost all criminal defendants) and gave them a right to a lawyer in a criminal case. As a result, Lehigh County Court suddenly had to find lawyers for hundreds of people who couldn't afford them.

The Lehigh County Bar rallied to solve the problem and did so, as most groups do, by using the dues of its older members and the sweat of new members. It hired two paid Public Defenders in 1965 at a total cost of $9,500 and required the six youngest members to serve as volunteer defenders to support them. In practice, if you were a new inductee, that meant you had to put in two weeks in court four times a year and represent anyone the law dragged in who had no money. Your service went on until another pack of new admittees took your place, usually in the following year. Most of the clients had been in criminal court before. I hadn't. Although I had been admitted in courtroom 1 of Lehigh County in December of the previous year, that had been a ten-minute ceremony. Since that time, I had spent my legal career in the lofty heights of the Pennsylvania Supreme Court as a law clerk. Now I sat, with my other five junior lawyer colleagues, in the lawyers' row of seats up front beyond the rail in courtroom 1.

President Judge Kenneth H. Koch was presiding. There is a thing about names in Pennsylvania Dutch counties. Everyone gets a very formal name which they carefully use throughout their lives. Everyone also gets a nickname from their young friends. The nickname also sticks. Judge Koch was, therefore, known as "Kenny" to my uncles and father. The Dutch like nicknames ending in a y sound. That September day, however, he was Judge Koch to me.

Kenneth H. Koch was kind to me throughout my career, always available to give me his advice and counsel and most understanding about my fumbles in his courtroom. He was, however, very much a man of the 1950s. Stolid, bald, with those plastic black glasses we all wore, and a booming voice, he ran "his" courtroom and "his" courthouse the way president judges did in those days. A former district attorney himself, he had the assistant district attorneys in perpetual terror as he lashed them to move cases.

The proceeding unfolding before me, as I somehow learned, was Arraignment court. Judge Koch called it "the pit." Years past, the arraignment had been the beginning and end of most criminal cases. Unrepresented and unprepared defendants simply pled guilty, and were sentenced on the spot. That changed when Ernest F. "Ernie" Ritter was appointed as county's first public defender. Tall, ramrod straight, poker-faced and always prepared, Ernie stood like a rock with the flotsam and jetsam of humanity flowing over him, every session of criminal court demanding that all defendants have lawyers from our volunteer forces. Judge Koch backed him up on that to his great credit.

As a result, when a young blonde woman was brought up to the bench out of the nearby "bull pen" where prisoners were kept, Judge Koch looked over the indictment which the DA handed him, seemed puzzled by it, and asked, "Mr. Gross would you speak to this defendant?" Thus, I met Kathleen Hallman. Interviews with defendants were expected to last 10 minutes. They took place standing along the walls of courtroom 1 which was packed with other criminal defendants.

I went overtime because Kathy's story was a bit complicated. She was charged with a felony corrupting the morals of minors. Actually, she had been at a "salt and pepper party" in Allentown – young black men and young white women. Allentown citizens being offended at such a sight called the police who, upon arriving, found the group had alcohol at their party, but otherwise weren't doing anything particularly criminal. Creative, nonetheless, the police realized that all the black men were over 18, while they thought all the young white women were under 18. Thus, they charged the men with corruption for furnishing drinks to the women. Unfortunately for Kathy, she and one other girl were also over 18. The Allentown cops, ever the model of legal consistency, arrested her and her friend on the same charge.

Kathy had been in Lehigh County prison for some weeks before I met her (naturally she couldn't make bail), and she immediately struck me as a rather naïve passive young woman, hardly a corruptor of youth. Although my first year law school course in criminal law was unrelated to what was going on in the pit, the charge didn't seem right either. As a result, when my next 10 minutes were up, I signaled that we were ready to proceed, and my voice croaking with fear, took the bold leap by answering "not guilty" to Judge Koch's query as to how the defendant pled.

I had no clue what would happen next. My great terror was that Judge Koch would order me immediately to pick a jury. He was perfectly capable of doing that. He didn't. Instead, he ordered Kathy back to prison, and I talked to Ernie Ritter who advised filing a Motion to Quash the Indictment. I had never heard of that Motion, but cobbled something together, filed it and got the District Attorney's office's attention. Judge Koch also signaled his concern about the validity of the charges when the Motion came before him. That kind of signal from the presiding judge meant something needed to be done about the case. Serious discussions then started as to how the charges could be dropped.

A non-pros was the obvious answer. However, non-pros' didn't just happen in those days. Instead, the defendant also had to show she was headed in the right direction before she was released. Kathy solved that problem by enlisting in the Job Corps, and a non pros was finally approved.

Kathy was my first success as a lawyer. I never heard from her again, but given her motivation and new confidence when she left the courthouse, I was very sure she had made it. In fact, I often cited her to other defendants over the next six years as an example of what good things could also happen for them as well.

By then, I had gotten to like courtrooms and trials. After several years as a volunteer, I had landed one of the paid part-time positions ($5,200 per year) in the Public Defenders office. I tried armed robbery, burglary and other serious felony cases. I fought appeals in the Superior Court and got some of Lehigh County's more egregious violations of the Constitution stopped. I even convinced the Supreme Court to reverse a murder conviction and got a few jury acquittals. It was a challenging and rewarding job most of the time.

Still by the early 1970s, I was feeling what would now be called burnout. First, the community attitude towards public defenders had changed drastically. There was something heroic about the idea that everyone had a right to counsel in the mid 1960s. People were interested in what I was doing and generally supportive when I explained how it all worked. Then the drug epidemic hit. Drug addicts flooded the town and courts. Car break-ins, petty burglaries and muggings became common, and we had to represent the defendants in most cases. We became pariahs—lawyers who delayed justice with silly motions about constitutional rights, who sometimes got "guilty" people off.

There was a second problem as well. I didn't like my new druggie clients. The old-fashioned career criminals who I had been representing were tough cookies. They knew what the legal world was like. They gave it no quarter. But, they asked none either. They wanted either the best trial they could get or the best plea bargain to shorten another stay in prison. That was it.

The drug addicts were totally different. They were slaves to their habit, and nothing in life mattered except heroin. As a result, according to them, nothing was their fault. I felt more like a social worker than a lawyer during those days.

Then came *Commonwealth v. Williams*; by the early 1970s we had moved the legal system to the point where the police could not interview defendants who wanted a lawyer. As a result, public defenders were on-call nights and weekends. I got such a call in 1971 to go down to Allentown Police Headquarters because Roy Williams had been arrested for murder.

When I arrived, I met a powerfully built professional boxer being held in the lock-up. The lead detective told me Roy had attacked and killed his wife with a machete in downtown Allentown. It had happened on a public street. There were a number of witnesses.

I got some basic facts from Roy, and then met with the police to find out the details of the crime. I knew these cops well. We trusted each other from years in court, so they had no trouble sharing their evidence with me, including a photograph of the dead victim. It was Kathy Hallman. The victim's side of the criminal justice system hit me in the face with that photo.

Defending Roy Williams was my ultimate personal and professional challenge, but I did it. After a long bitter trial, in which the district attorney constantly held up the machete for the jury to see, I managed to avoid a death sentence for him. Then I quit.

However, I didn't think that awful ending to my public defender career made what we did by starting the County's Public Defender system a failure. In a few short years we had changed the legal world here. From a revolving door of guilty pleas, we made the system deliver on its long hidden promise of a really fair proceeding for all rather than the very few who could afford to pay a lawyer.

Today, the Public Defender system is professionalized and largely full time. That provides better service to those represented. But for me and my colleagues who did it all for those few years when things were getting off the ground, it was a tremendous experience. My work as a public defender forced me to meet with and at least come to some understanding of the large mass of our citizens who are not only poor, but for most of their lives live inside our criminal justice system as defendants and victims. It gave me a perspective on life that was totally different from my middle-class upbringing.

Our Bar not only funded the public defender's system until the legislature finally recognized its obligation to do so, it also forced and shamed its newest members into giving the poor at least some representation. The Bar also did something else. It responded to the constitutional challenge of *Gideon v. Wainwright*. It went public in Allentown, defending and explaining why people needed a lawyer and why the criminal justice system could only work if defendants have a lawyer. That took real courage.

Two Mayors and a Lawyer

BIOGRAPHY-IN-BRIEF

Attorney Malcolm J. Gross was born October 2, 1940 in Allentown, Pennsylvania. He is a founding and senior partner in the Allentown law firm of Gross McGinley, LLP. He is the son of the late Allentown Mayor (1959-1964) John T. "Jack" Gross. His deceased grandfather Malcolm W. Gross also served as Mayor of the city from 1920-1932 and 1936-1940.

He earned his B.A. from Muhlenberg College, graduating cum laude in 1962, then earned his law degree from Villanova University School of Law in 1965. Among his many honors is inclusion in Pennsylvania Super Lawyers in 2004, 2006, and 2013, a distinction awarded to only five percent of Pennsylvania's top attorneys.

Mr. Gross has an extensive background as a lecturer and writer of history and social commentary. A lecturer at Cedar Crest College, he also serves as a member of the adjunct faculty at Muhlenberg College. He lectures frequently to civic and professional groups.

He has written for numerous publications including, *The Pennsylvania Law Weekly, Pennsylvania Lawyer* and *The Proceedings of the Lehigh County Historical Society.* He authored numerous op-eds for *The Morning Call* over a 25-year period.

In addition to his passion for law and public history he has an extensive background in supporting charitable organizations. He serves on the Board of Trustees of the Da Vinci Science Center where he was recently elected to the Executive Committee, and the Lehigh County Historical Society. He is also a current Chairman and Trustee of the esteemed Harry C. Trexler Trust of Lehigh County.

His community service spans nearly five decades. He has held numerous positions of leadership. He is a founder and former President of the Wildlands Conservancy; a former Chairman of Lehigh Valley Public Television WLVT-TV Channel 39; a former President of the Lehigh County Historical Society; former President of Lehigh Valley Child Care of Community Services For Children; the Allentown Symphony Orchestra Association and Board Member of Sacred Heart Hospital. Over the years he has served on numerous other Boards of nonprofit charitable institutions.

Presidents of the
Lehigh County Historical Society

1904-1917 ....George Taylor Ettinger, PhD
1918-1919 ....Charles Rhoads Roberts
1920-1926 ....The Rev. C. J. Cooper, DD
1927-1928 ....Robert G. Kleckner, Esquire
1929-1930 ....William F. Schlecter
1930-1944 ....Judge Frank M. Trexler
1945-1963 ....William J. Wilcox, Esquire
1963-1966 ....Melville J. Boyer, LHD
1966-1969...Eleanore Leh
1969-1972...Scott A. Trexler
1972-1973...John K. Heyl
1973-1974...Scott A. Trexler
1974-1976...David K. Bausch
1976-1978...Abram Samuels
1978-1980 ....William J. Albert
1980-1983...A. Newton Bugbee, Jr.
1983-1986 ....Richard W. Schaffer, Esquire
1986-1989 ....Edwin R. Baldrige, PhD
1989-1990 ....William H. Hacker, Sr.
1990-1993 ....Kurt D. Zwikl
1993-1996 ....Timothy S. Fallon
1996-1997 ....David A. Donio
1997-2000 ....Robert M. McGovern, Jr.
2000-2002 ....Glenn D. Koch
2002-2005 ....Raymond E. Holland
2005-2007 ....Robert G. Tallman, Esquire
2007-2009 ....Malcolm Gross, Esquire
2009-2011 ....Charles ("Chuck") Kelly
2011-2013 ....William H. Hacker, Jr.
2013-...Sonya Siegfried

A Brief History of the Lehigh County Historical Society

The Lehigh County Historical Society (LCHS) was founded in 1904 to preserve the history of Lehigh County, Pennsylvania. From our start as a research library, the Historical Society has grown to include our Lehigh Valley Heritage Museum and other historical properties, which include the 1770 Colonial Stone Mansion Trout Hall, the 1756 Troxell-Steckel Farm Museum in Whitehall Township, and the 1893 Claussville One-room Schoolhouse. LCHS also assists three county owned historical sites: 1893 Coplay Cement Kilns, 1868 Lock Ridge Furnace, and ca. 1850 Haines Mill. Collectively our historical properties help to tell the Lehigh Valley story of American history.

The 30,000 square foot Heritage Museum is a major repository. Our collections include 30,000 artifacts, over 80,000 vintage photographs and 3 million historical documents; the research library contains more than 11,000 rare books of local history.

The Heritage Museum devotes 13,000 square feet to exhibit space where changing exhibitions help bring history to life. Our exhibitions, public programs, school outreach and educational services to the community inspire civic ideals and historical literacy in children.

The Lehigh County Historical Society is a non-profit federally approved educational institution. We rely on the financial support of over 1,650 members and friends. Through membership dues, fundraising appeals, and estate bequests of stocks, and other assets, the Society operates because of the financial support of everyday people. Consider joining our *Legacy Society*. You can make a bequest in your Will or Estate Plan that will be recognized with your name displayed in our Heritage Museum.

You can enrich the next generation of children by helping us teach the lessons of history.

Two Mayors and a Lawyer